I0821240

BANG!

The Art, History, and Science of Fireworks

Ron Miller

TWENTY-FIRST CENTURY BOOKS / MINNEAPOLIS

This book is dedicated to Riverson, Forrest, River, and Airis.

Twenty-First Century Books™
An imprint of Lerner Publishing Group, Inc.
241 First Avenue North
Minneapolis, MN 55401 USA

For reading levels and more information, look up this title at www.lernerbooks.com.

Main body text set in ITC Novarese Std.
Typeface provided by Adobe Systems.

Library of Congress Cataloging-in-Publication Data

Names: Miller, Ron, 1947– author
Title: Bang! : the art, history, and science of fireworks / Ron Miller.
Other titles: Art, history, and science of fireworks
Description: Minneapolis : Twenty-First Century Books, [2026] | Includes bibliographical references and index. | Audience: Ages 11–18 | Audience: Grades 7–9 | Summary: "Explore the history and modern usage of fireworks, including how they were invented, how they are manufactured, the variety available, how people use them in holidays and cultural events, and more"—Provided by publisher.
Identifiers: LCCN 2025017289 (print) | LCCN 2025017290 (ebook) | ISBN 9798765660447 lib. bdg. | ISBN 9798765682937 epub
Subjects: LCSH: Fireworks—Juvenile literature
Classification: LCC TP300 .M55 2026 (print) | LCC TP300 (ebook) | DDC 662/.1—dc23/eng/20250908

LC record available at https://lccn.loc.gov/2025017289
LC ebook record available at https://lccn.loc.gov/2025017290

Manufactured in the United States of America
1-1012837-53637-8/28/2025

Contents

Introduction

The Art of Fire

This book is all about pyrotechnics. The word *pyrotechnics* comes from two Greek words: *pyro*, meaning "fire," and *techne*, meaning "art." *The art of fire*. In this book, we'll be examining the word to include almost anything related to pyrotechnics that is not meant to be used as a weapon. This includes not just the pyrotechnics we are all most familiar with—fireworks displays during holidays and other special events—but things we might not normally associate with fireworks, such as kitchen matches, roadside flares, and automobile airbags. Pyrotechnics is also an important part of many cultures and religions.

A person who works with pyrotechnics—either making them or using them—is a pyrotechnician. The most familiar type of pyrotechnician is a person who designs, sets up, and manages fireworks displays, such as the kind you might see during the Fourth of July or at a theme park or rock concert. Other pyrotechnicians create special effects for movies: everything from exploding buildings to re-creating volcanoes, smoke, and bullet impacts.

Chapter 1 The Origin of Fireworks

Unlike the history of the universe at large, the story of fireworks probably began with a little bang. Many legends and stories are about the origin of fireworks. One of them tells us that around 600 to 900 CE, a Chinese alchemist had been preparing a mixture of saltpeter, sulfur, honey, and other ingredients to create a special compound meant to prolong human life. The alchemist heated the substance to blend the ingredients, then let their attention wander for a moment . . . and *bang*! The substance burst into flame. This substance is called huoyao in Chinese, or "fire drug." It later became known as black powder, or gunpowder.

Other early stories talk about baozhu, or "exploding bamboos," the first natural fireworks. These were made by cutting a stalk of bamboo into sections and tossing them onto a fire. The moisture in the bamboo would turn to steam, causing the bamboo sections to explode. At the time, Chinese people believed these loud explosions warded off evil spirits. It didn't take much for people to realize that stuffing these traditional noisemakers with black powder would make them even noisier. Over time, bamboo tubes were replaced with small, tightly rolled paper tubes. These were much easier to make in large quantities.

Another legend attributes the invention of fireworks—or specifically, firecrackers—to Li Tian, a Chinese crafter and monk who lived during the Tang dynasty (618–907 CE) in the city of Liuyang. A statue was erected in his honor there, and the area is considered to be not only the birthplace of fireworks but the center of today's Chinese fireworks industry. Every year on April 18, citizens celebrate the invention of the firecracker. People give offerings in Li Tian's memory at a temple that the local people built during the Song dynasty (960–1279 CE) to honor him. In 2002 Liuyang also became the permanent headquarters of the International Fireworks Association.

Whatever their origin, fireworks became enormously popular. By the twelfth century, people had stabilized the proportions of ingredients in fireworks, which remain virtually the same today. The manufacture

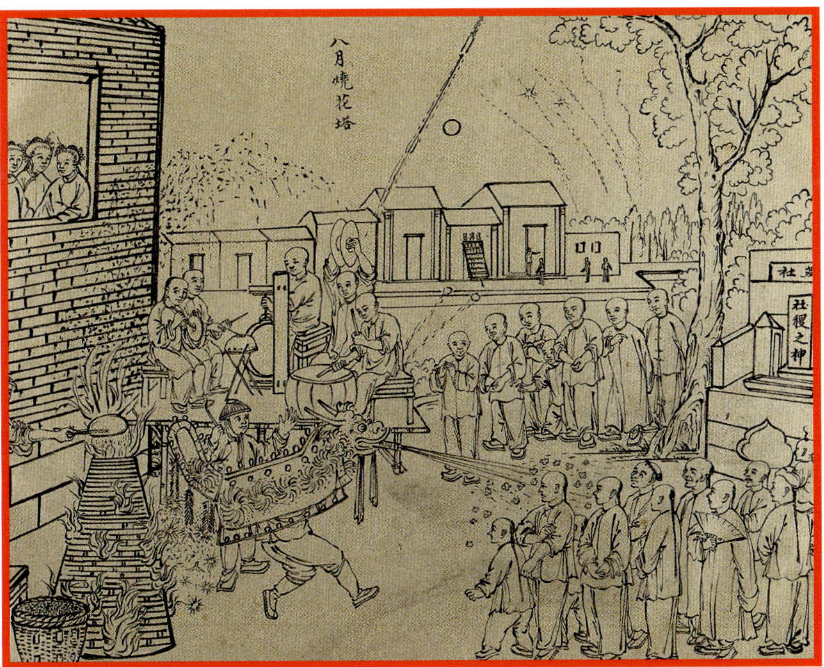

A nineteenth-century illustration of a public event in China. Fireworks have long served as everyday tools as much as celebratory features there.

and display of fireworks became an art form, and people held beautiful public exhibitions to admire them. Called yanhuo (smokes and fires), these fireworks were created for entertainment. An enormous variety of yanhuo were developed during and after the twelfth century, ranging from tiny firecrackers for children to enormously elaborate and complex structures for festivals or celebrations. Occasionally, such developments were more entertaining than anyone had anticipated. One popular firework was a "ground rat" (di lao shu), which was designed to race across the ground in an unpredictable course. This firework, one of the earliest ever created, can still be found in China nearly one thousand years later.

The Essential Ingredient

Black powder is the heart and soul of fireworks. Unfortunately, like many great human inventions, its origins are lost in antiquity and speculation. The story of the scorched alchemist that starts this chapter is likely simply a legend. Even so, records show that by 300 CE, a Chinese scientist named Ge Hong had already written down the ingredients of black powder and described its effects.

One of the three main ingredients of traditional black powder—saltpeter (potassium nitrate)—is found naturally in large quantities in China and India. It is a white, crystalline substance that can be collected from the floors and walls of caves. Saltpeter forms when bat droppings and decaying vegetation, which are rich in nitrogen compounds, get dissolved by rainwater and deposited on surfaces, such as the floors and walls of caves. These crystals were once useful in curing, or preserving, meat. Perhaps some time in the distant past someone accidentally dropped a portion of meat covered in saltpeter into a cooking fire. Instead of sizzling, the meat burst into flame. Further experimentation revealed that combining saltpeter with flammable substances made them burn much faster.

Saltpeter is easily combustible because the potassium nitrate molecule within it contains oxygen that it easily releases. This quality makes saltpeter an important ingredient in black powder. Saltpeter is the source of oxygen necessary for combustion. Black powder's second ingredient was originally honey. But people eventually discovered that charcoal was a more convenient fuel source—and cheaper.

The final key ingredient of black powder is sulfur. Alchemists likely discovered this during their search for both improved medicines and the philosopher's stone—an elusive substance that they incorrectly believed would turn material into gold—when they began experimenting with substances such as sulfur and charcoal. Since sulfur ignites easily, it burns first. The heat from the burning sulfur separates the oxygen from the saltpeter, and this in turn burns the charcoal and remaining sulfur. All this can happen very quickly. A train of ordinary black powder that is 1 inch (2.5 cm) long will burn completely in as little as 0.13 milliseconds (a millisecond is 0.001 of a second).

Perhaps some time in the distant past someone accidentally dropped a portion of meat covered in saltpeter into a cooking fire. Instead of sizzling, the meat burst into flame.

Early Pyrotechnics in the West

Incendiary devices have been a part of the arsenals in Western nations for nearly three thousand years. But almost all of them were intended for military use. Assyrian soldiers threw boiling pitch, a tarlike substance, on their enemies. Meanwhile, Greek armies launched firepots, or pots filled with combustibles, and flaming arrows and lances at their attackers. In 390 CE Roman writer Flavius Vegetius wrote about the use of an incendiary mixture of sulfur, resin, bitumen (a tarlike substance), and rope fibers all soaked in petroleum. This mixture would stick to anything it landed on and burn the object. Also, in the fourth century, Roman recordkeeper Claudius described what may have been the first public display of fireworks for entertainment: "twisting and turning globes of fire" that "ran about in different directions over the planks without burning or charring them."

A Roman ship turns Greek fire on their enemies at sea. Greek fire was popular in naval warfare because it could continue to burn on water.

Greek fire, a particularly violent type of incendiary, was first introduced to warfare when an Arab fleet attacked Constantinople in 673 CE. Although the fire's exact composition was kept secret, it was apparently a jellylike material made from sulfur, resin, and pitch dissolved in petroleum. This could be thrown in clay pots or ejected in a burning stream by a pump, much like the modern flamethrower.

But none of these weapons—as spectacular as they must have been—were *explosive.* Instead, they simply burned very quickly and very hot.

The Spread of Saltpeter

By the thirteenth century, the ability of saltpeter to support combustion was well known to Arab alchemists, who had learned of the chemical from Chinese researchers. The Arab writer Ibn al-Baytar, who died in 1248 CE, referred to saltpeter as "Chinese snow" and suggested that ancient Egyptian physicians had already been aware of it. This knowledge also began to spread in Europe.

In the thirteenth century, two Europeans, German scientist Albertus Magnus and English philosopher Roger Bacon, began their own research and experimentation with saltpeter, and recorded several formulas for explosive powders.

Bacon was different from other alchemists around this time. He championed the scientific method and insisted that all theories be tested before being accepted. Bacon was not satisfied to describe a phenomenon or idea—he performed experiments. This included experimenting with black powder.

Roger Bacon lived between 1220 and 1292. In addition to his work on black powder, he proposed various machines such as aircraft and motorized carriages.

Between 1257 and 1265, Bacon described the manufacture of black powder. He wrote, "Annis Arabum 630. . . . Item pondus totum sit 30. Sed tamen sal petrae LURU VOPO VIR CAN VTRIET sulphuris; et sic facies tonitruum et coruscationem, si scias artificium." This can be roughly translated as "Thou shalt take saltpeter LURU VOPO VIR CAN VTRIET and sulfur and by this means make thunder and lightning."

The part researchers were unclear on, of course, was the strange combination of letters in the middle. Researchers assumed this was an anagram—a word, phrase, or name formed by rearranging the letters of another. Many early scientists announced important discoveries this way since it allowed them to establish their precedence without revealing any secrets. As researchers later found out, the letters in Bacon's writing could be rearranged to disclose the recipe for black powder as seven parts saltpeter, five parts hazelwood charcoal, and five parts sulfur.

Bacon also described black powder in less uncertain terms. For example, he wrote in his book *Opus Majus*, "From the force of the salt called saltpeter so horrible a sound is produced by the bursting of so small a thing, namely, a small piece of parchment, that we perceive it exceeds . . . the greatest brilliancy of the lightning." And in the *Opus Tertium* he stated that "by the flash and combustion of fires, and by the horror of sounds, wonders can be wrought, and at any distance that we wish—so that a man can hardly protect himself or endure it." From these descriptions, historians could infer that Bacon not only knew what black powder could do but that he was making his own and trying it out. Possibly, the small pieces of parchment he was detonating might be considered the first firecrackers in the Western Hemisphere.

"By the flash and combustion of fires, and by the horror of sounds, wonders can be wrought, and at any distance that we wish—so that a man can hardly protect himself or endure it."
—Roger Bacon

Other scientists, such as Albertus Magnus, did not practice the scientific method as Bacon did but still made headway in understanding black powder. Albertus was the eldest son of a wealthy German lord. He was later given the name Magnus (meaning "great") in recognition for his work in philosophy and science. After studying liberal arts at the University of Padua, in Padua, Italy, he joined the Dominican order, one of the four major orders of the Catholic Church, which allowed him to study and teach wherever he pleased. Around 1241 CE, he read the books of Greek philosopher Aristotle and Arab scientists such as Omar Khayyam and Nasir al-Din al-Tusi, where he learned about the existence of gunpowder. Albertus spread his new knowledge throughout Europe. While in Paris, France, he began his great encyclopedic work, *De Mirabilibus Mundi* (The Wonders of the World), in which he endeavored to record the entire body of human knowledge. The book came out in the mid- to late 1200s. In it, he recorded a recipe for black powder.

Albertus's recipe was very similar to another recipe that appeared around that time, so some people speculate that he may have copied it directly. Around 1270 CE Byzantine author Marcus Graecus published a six-page treatise *The Liber Ignium ad Comburendos Hostes*, or "The Book of Fire for Burning up the Enemy." This contained thirty-five recipes for various Greek incendiary devices dating from 750 CE to the end of the 1200s CE. One of these recipes directed the reader to take "one pound [0.45 kg] of native sulfur, two pounds [0.9 kg] of linden or willow charcoal, six pounds [2.7 kg] of saltpeter, which three things are very finely powdered on a marble slab. Then put as much powder as desired into a case to make flying fire or thunder. Note.—The case for flying fire should be narrow and long and filled with well-pressed powder. The case for making thunder should be short and thick and half-filled with the said powder and at each end strongly bound with iron wire."

The writings and experiments of Bacon, Albertus, and Marcus led to an immediate widespread use of black powder throughout Europe. Militaries, in particular, embraced black powder, employing it in guns and bombs. For example, saltpeter improved Greek fire. Adding saltpeter turned Greek fire into an explosive mixture, capable of damaging ships and buildings and of propelling projectiles such as rockets far beyond the previous range.

Chapter 2

Fireworks as Art

While black powder was being quickly adopted as a weapon in the West, in other parts of the world, people mixed it with chemicals to create different-colored flames and other effects for entertainment. People in China, Japan, and India were the first to enjoy fireworks as works of art. Soon Europeans began enjoying their own fireworks displays.

Fireworks in Europe

One of the earliest known displays of fireworks in the West was in England in 1486 to celebrate the wedding of King Henry VII to Elizabeth of York. Another early fireworks show was during the coronation of Queen Anne Boleyn, the second wife of King Henry VIII, in 1533. A century later, Czar Peter the Great of Russia arranged a spectacular show that lasted for five hours to celebrate the birth of his son.

Still, until about the sixteenth century, fireworks displays were not very common in Europe. There were no written records of a public fireworks display before the 1500s, and later records show that very few of the fireworks shows in Europe were strictly for public amusement. Most were created to impress royal visitors or guests.

Fireworks Take Off in England

By Queen Elizabeth I's reign from 1559–1603, fireworks displays that weren't solely part of royal celebrations were becoming more common. Elizabeth I appeared to be partial to fireworks. Throughout her reign, she held displays on many occasions and seemingly on the slightest excuse. For example, fireworks were often used in mock battles to simulate cannon fire, guns, and bombs, or even thunder and lightning.

Stage plays also employed fireworks to improve the audience's experience. English playwright William Shakespeare (1564–1616) made several references to fireworks in his plays, such as *Henry VIII* or *Love's Labor's Lost*, where the character Armado says, "The King would have me present the Princess . . . with some delightful . . . show . . . or firework."

Fireworks had grown so popular in England that by 1635 author John Bate published a manual for the creation of fireworks, *The Second Booke, Teaching Most Plainly, and Withall Most Exactly the Composing of all Manner of Fire-Works for Tryumph and Recreation*. It was one of the first books to be published in English with a special section devoted to fireworks. Mathematician John White published *The Art of Ringing* in the late 1600s. The second part of this book, *Artificial Fireworks*, contained detailed instructions on how to create fireworks, from molds to other parts of the process. Fireworks became such an important part in royal events that King James II knighted his royal fire master, or pyrotechnician, for the spectacular show he created for James II's 1685 coronation.

By then, fireworks had grown so wildly popular that the government passed laws restricting their sale and usage to reduce injuries, fires, and noise. King William III (1650–1702) passed a law that declared, "If any person shall make or sell any fireworks, or implements for making the same, he shall, on conviction before one justice, or chief magistrate, by confession, or by oath of two witnesses, forfeit 5 [pounds] to the poor." The law was still in force in 1780 when a man named Richard Roundson was fined £5 for "throwing squibs, serpents, and other fireworks."

Green Men

Historically, men who performed with handheld fireworks were described as green men. This was because they covered their bodies with fresh leaves to protect themselves from being burned by flying sparks. In 1610 an account of a fireworks display described "two men in green ivy, set with work upon their other habit, with black hair and black beards, very ugly to behold, and garlands upon their heads, with great clubs in their hands, with fireworks to scatter abroad to maintain the way for the rest of the show." John Bate also described the clubs the green men used in his 1635 manual. The title page of the manual (*right*) even features an illustration of one of these green men.

THE
SECOND BOOKE
Teaching moſt plainly, and withall
moſt exactly, the compoſing of all
manner of Fire-works for Tryumph
and Recreation.

By IOHN BATE.

LONDON,
Printed by *Thomas Harper* for *Ralph Mab.*
1635.

John Bate's fireworks manual was part of his compendium *The Mysteries of Nature and Art*. The section on fireworks opened on an illustration of a green man.

The Field in France

In France, King Louis XIV seemed to be as enthusiastic about fireworks as Elizabeth I. During his reign from 1638–1715, French pyrotechnicians made great advances in their field. One particularly fine display of fireworks held in 1669 inspired the engineer and

Paris, France, puts on a fireworks show every year to celebrate Bastille Day, a holiday celebrating an event important to the French Revolution (1789–1794) **(see page 76).**

mathematician Amédée-François Frézier to write a treatise on pyrotechnics, called *Traité des Feux d'artifice pour le Spectacle*, which he published in 1706. He also established a workshop to manufacture fireworks. Frézier emphasized the creation of fireworks for recreation, ceremonies, and entertainment. He was one of the first people to consider the possibility of pyrotechnics being a form of art in the West.

The fireworks spectacles staged by the French monarchy enabled it to judge the political temperature of the nation, while providing its subjects with unmatched entertainment and a feeling of goodwill toward their rulers in much the same way the emperors of Rome entertained their citizens with games held in the Coliseum.

Italian Innovation

One of the reasons why France made so much progress in pyrotechnics was due to King Louis XV (1710–1774). Louis XV encouraged five brothers from Italy, a country that was a major player in the development of fireworks in the West, to advance the field. These brothers were Antonio, Francesco, Gaetano, Petronio, and Pietro Ruggieri. The Ruggieri family was a well-known and established Italian family dedicated to pyrotechnics as an art form.

Louis XV invested large sums of money on fireworks displays as they were a symbol of nobility and the military. Displays in France during the eighteenth century were largely devoted to celebrating births among the nobility and great military victories. One of the finest of these fireworks displays took place at Versailles Palace in 1739. Petronio Ruggieri's son, Claude Fortune Ruggieri, was in charge of its production. In 1821 Claude Fortune's own son, Désiré-François Ruggieri, wrote: "There appeared for the first time the Salamander la Rosace and le Guilloche, which are still admired today." The Salamander la Rosace and le Guilloche were the names of specific pyrotechnic displays. The first got its name, which translates to the "Salamander Rosette," from a legend that a salamander—a small, lizardlike amphibian—could survive burning in a fire. The word *salamander* came to be applied to anything used in connection with fire. The second, le Guilloche, got its name due to the firework display's elaborate ribbonlike appearance of the fiery effect. A guilloche is an architectural design that looks like braided ribbons.

The Ruggieri family was known for adding colors to their fireworks. At the time, fireworks typically only exploded in flashes of white, yellow, and orange. But the Ruggieris introduced colors such as red, blue, and green by adding different chemical elements to black powder. Orange was the standard color of burning black powder. Adding sodium to black powder resulted in a bright yellow flash. Aluminum or magnesium powder gave a bright white flash of light. Copper turned the flash blue, and iron filings resulted in bright gold sparks. Meanwhile, strontium produced a red flash, and barium resulted in green.

Fireworks Masterpieces

The first European people to make headway in pyrotechnics as an art form were likely Italians. During the Renaissance (1400–1600), artists trained at pyrotechnic schools across Europe, particularly in Italy. The peninsula nation was famous for its elaborate and colorful displays. Amid great works by artists such as the painter Leonardo da Vinci and the sculptor Michelangelo, pyrotechnicians perfected their art, developing new and ever more beautiful types of fireworks.

Aerial shells were one of these innovations. People launched shells high into the air before the shells burst with loud bangs, bright flashes, and showers of sparks. In 1610 military engineer Diego Ufano reported in his book *Artillery* that while only very simple fireworks were being made in Spain, magnificent spectacles had been seen in Italy more than fifty years earlier. In his 1540 book *De la Pirotechnia* (On Pyrotechnics), metalworker Vannoccio Biringuccio seems to confirm this by describing fireworks in the Italian cities of Florence and Vienna that were incorporated into elaborate constructions of wood up to 72 feet (22 m) high. When ignited, the fireworks could be seen for miles.

Thanks to the Ruggieris' contributions, as well as those from many other families, Italy remained a leader in the art of pyrotechnics until the mid-1800s.

Symbols and Mythos

Fireworks displays were often created by royal engineers or engineers employed by cities. Many of these engineers were free to design their creations without being bound by any special political or social agenda. Their patrons' main concern was simply achieving something spectacular. Fireworks engineers often drew upon current events—such as the birth or death of someone in a royal family or perhaps a great military victory. They were also inspired by mythology.

In 1638 pyrotechnician Thomas Caresme erected a vast allegorical sculpture on the Seine River to celebrate the birth of King Louis XIV. He designed the display so that a rock was constructed on top of a high scaffolding and above this, a rising sun—symbolizing the newborn heir. On the four sides of the structure stood allegorical figures representing Peace, Science, Harmony, and Abundance. Later, royal pyrotechnicians would draw influence from individual artists, poets, authors, and sculptors to make fireworks displays even grander and more theatrical.

Eventually, fireworks displays began to take on the political concerns of royalty. From that moment, according to French historian Émile Magne, "fireworks displays, formerly so diversified in their form, tend to take on the definite image of a monument, a temple, an arch of triumph. . . . No more romanticism, chimerical adventures, unexpected scenes."

Firing Off in Northeastern Europe

Although Italy and France dominated the fireworks scene for several centuries, they had no claim on exclusivity in Europe. A book published in the Netherlands in 1780, *Beschrijving van Kunst Vuurwerken* (A Description of the Art of Fireworks), was filled with detailed colored illustrations of the tools pyrotechnicians used, as well as numerous special fireworks effects such as skyrockets, Catherine wheels (small, rocketlike fireworks attached to a wheel, which spins rapidly when ignited), and more. Germany was fond of fireworks, as was Sweden. As in other parts of Europe, many of these countries' displays were associated with royal events such as marriages, births, and deaths. In one event in 1697, a thousand skyrockets were fired. The cost of these and the other fireworks fired that night was £12,000—equivalent to $4 million today.

Special Events

The practice of celebrating special events and occasions with fireworks was not universally popular. Nineteenth-century British author

Brocks Fireworks

In 1698 John Brock founded Brocks Fireworks, a fireworks manufacturing company. The company is still in business and is one of the oldest companies in Great Britain. In 1826 Brocks Fireworks began holding public fireworks displays known as Brock's Benefits. The company frequently held shows at London's popular Crystal Palace exhibit hall, and those shows became so popular that Brock registered Crystal Palace Fireworks as a trademark. The Crystal Palace shows, which were open to the public, were held until the Crystal Palace burned down in 1936. The largest show the company ever produced celebrated the signing of the treaty that ended World War I (1914–1918).

Charles Lamb, for instance, complained about the damage fireworks did to London's Hyde Park when celebrations took place there and in Green Park. A reporter for *The Times* (London) complained that "the repetition of these things, with occasional pauses, for more than two hours became tedious to all." Both he and Lamb were in the minority. Fireworks bored few people. Despite some grumblings, fireworks drew large crowds throughout the 1800s.

In 1865 British pyrotechnician C. T. Brock of Brocks Fireworks inaugurated a series of impressive and immensely successful displays at the Crystal Palace. Following this, Brock began producing rockets and other pyrotechnic devices "on a scale never previously dreamt of in the trade."

One of the most ambitious fireworks spectacles in history was held in 1897 for Queen Victoria's Diamond Jubilee, a celebration in honor of her sixtieth year on the British throne. *Celebrations* might be a better word. Tons of fireworks were distributed to every corner of the British Empire, which at that time ruled up to a quarter of the world's

Advertisements for fireworks shows often featured illustrations of grand displays.

population, including more than 450 million people in territories in Canada, Australia, Africa, and India. People even hauled cases of fireworks by canoe nearly 400 miles (640 km) up the Zambezi River in Africa just so they could be distributed. They were then carried over land, with ten people needed to carry each case of fireworks. The fireworks were all set off on June 22, 1897.

Fireworks in America

European firework technology eventually spread to the Americas. In 1588 English astronomer and mathematician Thomas Harriot described showing "wildefire woorkes," or fireworks, to the Indigenous peoples of North America. Then, in 1624, Captain John Smith, governor of the New England colonies, recorded that on the evening of July 24, 1608, they lit a few rockets, which scared the Indigenous people and made them think that the colonists could do anything. After that, the Indigenous people decided to help the colonists.

These early fireworks had been brought to the New England colonies from England. But beginning in the 1700s, a local pyrotechnic industry was quickly taking shape in the colonies. People also began importing Chinese fireworks. These fireworks proved to be so popular that soon every ship making the journey from New England to India or China returned with firecrackers, along with tea, silk, and rice. Soon ships returned with skyrockets and other fireworks.

In 1776 the New England colonies split off from Great Britain and became the United States of America. The Boston Commons, a public park, was the site of the very first Fourth of July fireworks spectacle. Also called Independence Day, the Fourth of July celebrates the United States' independence from England. The Boston Commons remained the host of many of the most famous Fourth of July fireworks displays for many years. A centerpiece of the event is often a gigantic portrait of George Washington outlined in sparks and flames.

In the 1840s the *Independence*, a ship captained by US Captain Decimus Forthridge, was stranded off the coast of Sumatra, Indonesia. As a horde of Malay pirates attacked the ship, Forthridge found himself without ammunition to repel the invaders. But he did have a stock of fireworks he had taken on board to celebrate the coming Fourth of July. The captain and his crew used these fireworks to frighten off the invaders.

The American Civil War (1861–1865), fought between the Union and the Confederate States of America, brought many advancements in firearms and ammunition. Some of these advancements found their way into the development of pyrotechnics. For instance, so much gunpowder was required for guns and cannons that factories found ways to manufacture gunpowder on a large scale, which was then applied to the manufacture of fireworks.

People also celebrated the end of the Civil War with spectacular fireworks displays—probably none more elaborate than those held in New York on July 4, 1865. Organizers picked fourteen different locations throughout the city, designating each with its own program of displays. The themes ranged from patriotic to mythological, such as "Star of Independence," "Yankee Windmill," "Fairies Frolic," "Egyptian Pyramid," "Persian Rose," and "Temple of Liberty with Figure of Grant."

Martha Coston

Inventor Martha Coston was only twenty-one years old when her husband, Benjamin Franklin Coston, died. From some notes that Benjamin left, Martha created a system of flares that could be used by ships to communicate at night. The Costons' goal was to create flares that could create very pure red, green, and white light that distant ships could easily see. The flare was a specially designed gun, with cartridges of different colors. Handlers would use different combinations of colors to communicate different messages, using the numbers 0–9, as well as the letters *A* and *P*. For instance, a white flare indicates the number 1, while a red flare followed by green indicates the number 6. A flash of white, red, then white is the letter *P*; and a flash of red, white, and red is the letter *A*. The letter *P* is a preparatory signal. If the other party answers back with *A*, that means they have seen the preparatory signal, and you can begin your message. The signal 11, for instance, would mean "enemy to our front," while 31 would mean "cease firing."

The US government paid Coston $20,000 and initiated a contract to manufacture flares, and the US Navy adopted her flare system. During the Civil War, it gave the Union an advantage over the Confederate navy, which had no easy method for ships to communicate at night. Coston's flares are credited with being one of the deciding factors in the Union's eventual victory. The US Life-Saving Service (which became the US Coast Guard) also used Coston's flares to warn of dangerous conditions or to summon rescuers to ships in distress. The Coston Supply Company operated until the late 1970s, supplying flares for navies and shipping companies around the world.

From then on, fireworks were used to celebrate many major events in the history of the United States, from presidential inaugurations to the ending of wars. One major fireworks event celebrated the opening of the Brooklyn Bridge in New York on May 24, 1883. Heralded as one of the great engineering wonders of the world, the Brooklyn Bridge was the pride of a young nation showing off its abilities to the rest of the world. Huge crowds—with more than fifty thousand people arriving by train alone—came to hear the president's speech, watch a parade, and witness a grand fireworks display that evening. It was advertised as the largest fireworks show to be held in America up until that time, and rockets, fountains, and other effects were launched from the bridge and its twin towers.

Fireworks were used to celebrate many major events in the history of the United States, from presidential inaugurations to the ending of wars.

Part of the opening of the Brooklyn Bridge was a cannon firing to mark US President Chester A. Arthur and New York Mayor Franklin Edson crossing the bridge. But the biggest pyrotechnics display during the celebration was that night's fireworks show.

The Italian Connection

Many of the leading fireworks manufacturers and display designers in the United States came from Italy, where display fireworks were originally perfected by innovators such as the Ruggieris. Many families who had been practicing the art for generations immigrated to the United States during the 1800s. So many of these families eventually settled in the states of New York, New Jersey, Pennsylvania, Ohio, West Virginia, and Kentucky that this region became known as the fireworks belt.

The Grucci and Lanzetta families were two of the first to arrive in the US. Angelo Lanzetta had created a fireworks business in Italy in 1850 and brought it to America in 1910. Angelo's son, Anthony, continued the business after his father's death and invited his cousin, Felix Grucci Sr., to join the company. By the 1920s, Fireworks by Grucci was booming. It is now owned and managed by Felix Grucci, with his son, Christopher, representing the fifth generation of the family. With offices around the world, it produces hundreds of fireworks shows in the United States and other countries. On New Year's Eve in 2013, the company produced one of its largest shows, with 479,651 fireworks launched above the skyline of Dubai in the United Arab Emirates. In 2014 Fireworks by Grucci created another display for New Year's Eve in Dubai. Firing nearly 480,000 shells in just six minutes, it was the largest fireworks display ever.

The Zambelli family was another Italian family that brought their knowledge of fireworks to the United States. In 1893 pyrotechnic artist Antonio Zambelli arrived in the United States, along with his book of designs and formulas for all the special fireworks his family had developed. He soon created the Zambelli Fireworks Manufacturing Company in New Castle, Pennsylvania. The Zambellis have produced fireworks for every president since John F. Kennedy, earning the company the title: Zambelli, the First Family of Fireworks. The company is one of the largest fireworks

The Sorgi family assembling fireworks

manufacturers in the world, creating more than sixteen hundred shows every year.

Vincenzo Sorgi, a fourth-generation fireworks maker, immigrated to the United States in 1899, where he created the American Fireworks Company in 1902. The company produces both display fireworks for professional shows as well as consumer fireworks such as firecrackers, bottle rockets, fountains, and sparklers.

Augustine Santore began creating fireworks professionally in Italy in 1860. Santore moved to the United States in 1890. Along with his three sons, Augustine founded Fireworks by Santore that same year. The company has provided spectacular displays for events such as the annual Times Square New Year's Eve ball drop in New York as well as for venues such as Busch Gardens, the Daytona Speedway, and Walt Disney World.

Even more fireworks celebrated the one-hundredth anniversary of the bridge's opening. Fireworks by Grucci designed the display, and it was the largest event the company had ever created. "We're using everything," said Felix Grucci Jr., then president of the company, "Instead of a Broadway stage, we have the skyline of New York. It will be a theatrical performance in the sky." In a show lasting about thirty-five minutes, the team launched ninety-six hundred rockets, shells, fountains, and other effects from the bridge's roadway and two towers, as well as from three barges anchored in the river below. The Gruccis made a special effort to try to duplicate many of the effects from the fireworks display that had accompanied the original opening ceremony in 1883. One of the most striking of these was the "Cascade," a curtain of white fire falling from the entire length of the bridge's roadway.

Historically, the largest fireworks displays in the United States have been those that New York's Macy's department store company sponsors every Fourth of July. The fireworks are launched from a series of barges moored in the East River, near the Brooklyn Bridge. In 2022 fifty pyrotechnicians fired nearly two thousand shells and effects every minute during the two-hour show. But rivaling the Macy's fireworks show for largest show in the US is an event in Kentucky called Thunder over Louisville. Designed to kick off the Kentucky Derby every May, fireworks are launched from up to eight 400-foot-long (122 m) barges anchored in the Ohio River near the Second Street Bridge. Zambelli Fireworks (see sidebar on pages 26–27) designs the show and provides the fireworks. In 2018 an audience of over eight hundred thousand people witnessed more than sixty thousand

In 2022 fifty pyrotechnicians fired nearly two thousand shells and effects every minute during the two-hour Macy's Fourth of July show.

shells fired into the sky. Organizers also included a special half-hour show, including a "waterfall" of fireworks cascading from the length of the bridge.

Welcoming a New Century

Virtually every major city around the world celebrated the advent of a new millennium on New Year's Eve in 1999. Because midnight occurs at different times in different regions, the first city to officially celebrate the new century with fireworks was Auckland, New Zealand. About an hour later, Sydney, Australia, greeted the new year with midnight fireworks fired from its Harbour Bridge—an annual event inspired by the centennial celebration of the Brooklyn Bridge. Cities in Japan, China, Vietnam, and Greece all fired fireworks in celebration of the new year. In Paris, displays went off around the Eiffel Tower. In London, organizers created a "river of fire" along 4 miles (6.4 km) of the Thames River. They used 39 tons (35 t) of fireworks on sixteen barges, set to fire off in time with Earth's rotation. The idea was to create a wave of fire traveling up the river at a speed of 650 miles (1,046 km) per hour. A computer would set off bursting charges every 0.675 seconds. Unfortunately, no one could see the entire display from any one location since the barges were between 300 and 750 feet (95 and 230 m) apart.

As midnight crossed the Atlantic Ocean, pyrotechnicians launched fireworks from the Peace Tower in Ottawa, Canada. At the same time, fireworks displays began in cities along the American East Coast. The first town in the United States to greet the New Year was Lubec, Maine—the easternmost town in the country—which shot off a fireworks display over its harbor just before dawn. Boston, Massachusetts, followed with fireworks over Boston Harbor and the Commons. Chicago, Illinois, launched fireworks over Lake Michigan. Then Fairbanks, Alaska, greeted the New Year with fireworks. When midnight finally reached the Hawaiian Islands, Honolulu—Hawaii's capital city—set off their own fireworks. The last nation to enter the twenty-first century was Samoa with a final fireworks display.

Chapter 3

How Fireworks Are Made

Fireworks are manufactured all over the world. But because making fireworks is very labor-intensive—a great deal of the work must be done by hand—the countries that produce the most fireworks are typically those where labor is cheapest. China is the world's largest manufacturer and exporter of fireworks. In 2022 China accounted for 71 percent of the world's total fireworks exports, worth $1.29 billion, which is more than thirty times that of the next highest exporter, Germany. Fireworks are also made in India, the Netherlands, France, Poland, Brazil, and many other countries, including the United States.

Making Fireworks

Here is how one of the most familiar Fourth of July fireworks—the aerial shell—is made. In use, the aerial shell launches from a heavy tube and creates a loud thump. A trail of sparks soars into the sky. When it reaches its highest point, the shell explodes with a bang, and provides a beautiful display of bright sparks, flashes, crackling sounds, and many other exciting effects.

Behind the scenes at a large fireworks show are rows of the large mortars used to launch aerial effects.

The first ingredient in almost all fireworks is black powder. While the three main ingredients of black powder—saltpeter, sulfur, and charcoal—are by themselves largely harmless, they become dangerous when mixed, so workers must take great care. Only highly skilled workers should handle them.

Stars, comets, and other special effects are also part of aerial shells. Stars are the little explosives, or pellets, that create bright flashes of colored light, sparks, and sometimes loud bangs when a firework explodes in the sky. Comets are similar to stars, but instead of a bright flash or noise, they create long streamers of sparks when ignited. Without either stars or comets, the aerial shell would simply explode in a puff of smoke.

Both stars and comets are handmade in a factory. A worker uses a scale to carefully measure accurate amounts of every ingredient. These include oxidizers that supply oxygen for combustion, binders that help hold all the ingredients together, and chemicals that create the desired colors or noises when the firework explodes. The ingredients are similar to the coating on a sparkler (a metal rod coated with a flammable substance that creates a shower of bright sparks when lit). After combining certain powders together, workers then moisten the mixture to activate the binder. Once the binder is activated, it acts as a glue that holds all the ingredients together. The result is a kind of dough that might be spread out flat and cut into small cubes or other shapes. Or the dough might be rolled into long, snakelike ropes that can then be cut into small sections. The star or comet dough is then shaped into pellets. This is done by placing the dough into large tubs that resemble kitchen mixers. As the tubs rotate, the doughy mixture rolls and forms small balls. Once the stars or comets are shaped, they are left to dry.

Aerial Shell Containers

An aerial shell begins with a hollow container. To make this, a handler glues layers of paper together. Most shells are in the shape of hollow spheres, but they can come in canlike cylinders too. Technicians place stars in the shell. Then it is filled with rice hulls or husks that have been coated with black powder. This is the bursting or break charge—a small explosive charge that ignites and scatters the stars when the aerial shell reaches a certain height.

Shells start out in two pieces. After a spherical shell is filled, handlers glue the two halves together. If it is a cylindrical shell, then the top is glued onto the cylinder. To reinforce the shell so it doesn't fly apart when it's launched, workers wrap string around the shell, then glue another layer of paper over that.

The shell is then glued on top of the lifting charge. This is a small, paper-wrapped cylinder filled with black powder. When ignited, the lifting charge launches the shell into the air.

Fuses are used to set off fireworks. These are strings coated with black powder and then wrapped in paper. One fuse ignites the lifting charge that launches the shell. Another fuse inside the shell burns slowly as the shell is in flight, giving the shell time to reach its full altitude. Then it ignites the bursting charge, creating a beautiful display of fireworks in the sky.

Setting Off a Shell

Aerial shells are sometimes thought to be skyrockets, or a rocket designed to explode high in the sky, since they also leave a long trail of sparks behind as they fly into the air. Unlike skyrockets, aerial shells are fired from a kind of gun called a mortar. This is a heavy tube made of metal or fiberglass. The bursting charge itself often looks like a paper-wrapped ball sitting on top of a paper-wrapped cylinder that has a long fuse attached. The bursting charge is placed into the tube with the fuse hanging outside. The cylinder contains the lifting charge. When the fuse is lit, the lifting charge ignites, shooting the ball straight up into the air. At the time it's launched, a delay fuse is ignited. When the ball reaches its intended height, the delay fuse ignites the bursting charge. This ejects whatever special effect the shell might contain, perhaps stars or comets that rain down in a shower of sparks.

Mortars come in all sizes. Those available to the consumer are about 2 inches (5 cm) in diameter and about 8 to 15 inches (20 to 38 cm) long. The shells these mortars launch can reach a height of 50 to 75 feet (15 to 23 m) before exploding. Mortars used by professional pyrotechnicians

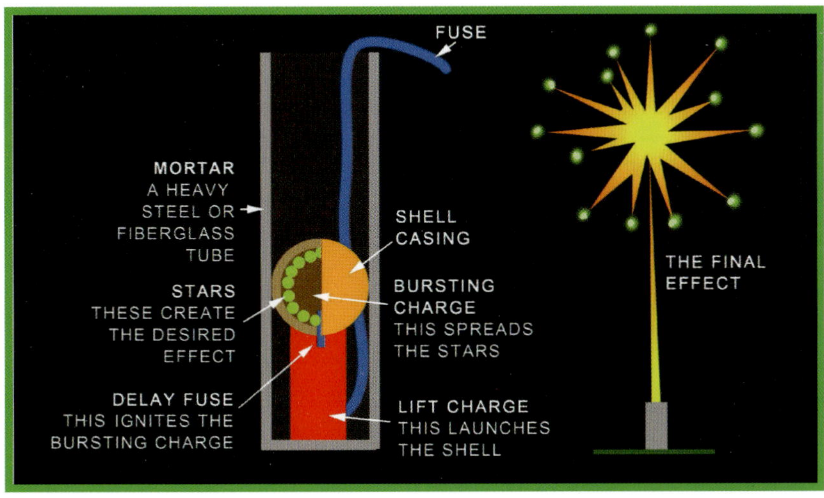

A cross-section of a mortar containing an aerial shell. The mortar contains the lifting and bursting charges, the fuses, and the shell casing, which holds the additional components, such as stars or comets, that determine what the firework will look like.

range from 3 to 24 inches (7.6 to 61 cm) in diameter, though they are typically between 6 and 12 inches (15 to 30 cm) in diameter.

Aside from size, there is no important difference between how consumer mortars and aerial shells work and those that professionals use.

Firecrackers

Firecrackers are a loud and explosive firework, typically wrapped in paper and lit with a fuse. They are usually small. They're also frequently bundled in a roll, connected by a fuse that sets off each firecracker in turn once lit. Firecrackers are probably the most popular of all consumer fireworks. They are simple and inexpensive to make, so they can be found around the world. You might find firecrackers sold in packs at some stores around the Fourth of July. But firecrackers are also dangerous if not handled carefully, so they are often regulated or sometimes banned in places where fireworks are controlled.

Many firecrackers are flashlight firecrackers. This means that flash powder is used instead of black powder. Flash powder contains aluminum or magnesium powder combined with potassium perchlorate, which acts as an oxidizer. When flash powder burns, it creates a louder bang than black powder. It also releases a flash of light.

To create a firecracker, workers add a small amount of black powder or flash powder into a paper tube. Until the 1900s, nearly all firecrackers were handmade in China by families working in shops set up in their homes. Most modern firecrackers available on the US market are still handmade in China—as are most fireworks—but in large factories rather than individual homes, which is much safer.

Fountains

Probably the most popular consumer firework is the gerb, or fountain. The fountain is also considered the simplest firework, since it is little more than a tube filled with black powder. Each fountain is enclosed in a cylindrical case, usually made of paper and held together by glue. Workers then add the explosive mixture into the case. This might consist of black powder combined with whatever special effects are desired.

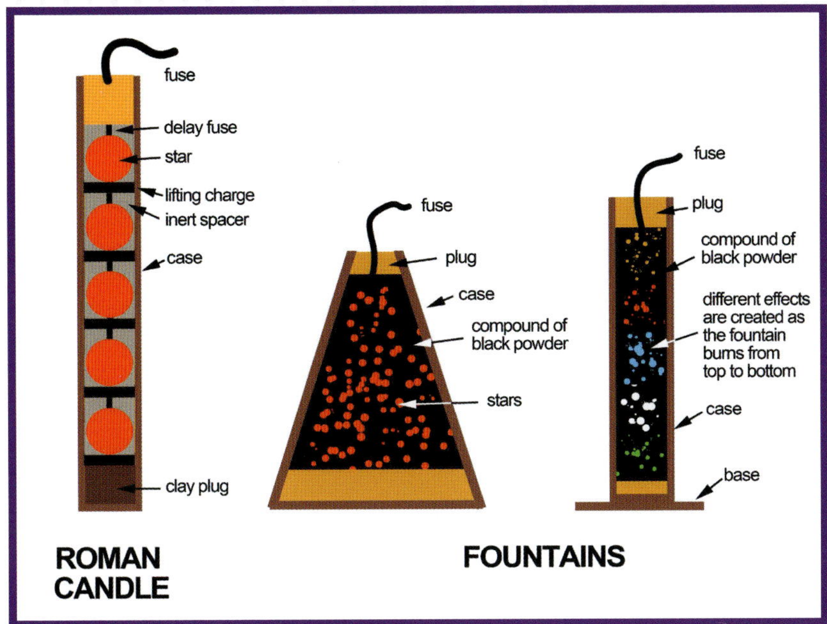

Roman candles contain several inert spacers to create delays between their effects. Fountains, on the other hand, contain mixtures that ignite and go off all at once.

For instance, someone might want to create small fireworks that set off colored sparks, smoke, or crackling sounds. Iron filings, for example, create bright yellow sparks. After a person has determined what effects they desire, they can produce a mixture that will create those effects. The mixture is then carefully pressed into the case with a wooden tool called a drift that fits the diameter of the case, so there is no space for air or the mixture to escape.

Set Pieces

Set pieces are fireworks that, when ignited, create a unique design such as a word, sentence, shape, company logo, or even a portrait of a person. They are the least displayed type of firework, due to how difficult and expensive it is to construct them. Set pieces have large frameworks, usually made of wood or rattan, which can be attached to any number of different kinds of fireworks. Set pieces are very similar to toritos and castillos, which are also fireworks attached to wooden frameworks, used to celebrate holidays in Mexico (see page 78).

Safety Precautions

Experienced professionals who pay a great deal of attention to safety make fireworks. The actual methods of making a firework have hardly changed in hundreds of years, but this is due less to tradition and more to safety concerns. Most fireworks—whether they're made for big outdoor displays or for consumers—are made entirely or mostly by hand. This is because machines always bring the risk of a stray spark setting off a supply of black powder and other chemicals. Still, modern machines can help. Some machines only mix the ingredients in black powder, and other machines carry out every stage in the manufacture of a firecracker, from creating the paper tube and filling it with black powder to inserting the fuse and attaching a label.

One of the first fireworks factories in China to employ machinery in making fireworks was the Zhongzhou Fireworks Group Co., Ltd., in Liuyang. Developers hoped that human-caused accidents could be reduced by limiting the amount of work that needed to be done by hand. The less human contact with black powder, the safer the process would be. Where three hundred employees were once needed to create the millions of firecrackers the company sold every year, only eleven are

Workers in some fireworks factories must carefully check that each firework contains the correct amount of black powder or flash powder. This helps make sure the firework and the factory are safe.

now needed. They take safety precautions to limit machine accidents. A limit of 50 pounds (23 kg) of black powder is spread across eighteen separate machines, all of which operate automatically. A closed system prevents any of the powder being exposed to air, so it can't access the oxygen needed to combust.

Zhongzhou Fireworks Group is one of the largest manufacturers of fireworks in China and can afford to install expensive automatic machinery. While this is still beyond the resources of the many smaller companies, more are following suit. Deaths in China related to fireworks manufacturing accidents fell from an annual average of 400 from 1986–2005 to 188 in 2009.

Companies take other steps to keep the creation of fireworks as safe as possible. Antistatic devices might be installed at the entrances and exits of buildings. These devices neutralize any static electricity that might be clinging to an employee, reducing the possibility of setting off accidental sparks. Employees may also wear antistatic overalls, shoes, socks, caps, and gloves. Cotton clothing is safer for employees to wear versus wool or silk since the latter two can generate static. They may also wear rubber-soled shoes and are careful not to wear anything made of metal.

Inside manufacturing halls, floors may be kept moist, and the relative humidity of the air must be kept above 60 percent. This also helps reduce static electricity, which forms more easily in dry air. Equipment is made of wood, bamboo, copper, or aluminum to reduce the chance of creating sparks. Similarly, employee tools are made of wood or brass. And all machinery and workbenches are grounded—a wire connects them with the ground. This drains off static charges similar to the way a lightning rod works to protect a house.

A typical fireworks factory doesn't look much like other factories from the outside. Instead of one large building, a fireworks factory may have dozens of small buildings scattered far apart over a wide area. For example, the American Fireworks Company occupies sixty buildings spread over 70 acres (28 ha) of Ohio countryside. Each building of a fireworks factory may be devoted to the making of a different type of

Setting Records

Fireworks can create amazing displays, and around the world, people are constantly finding new ways to make each event more special. Here are a few records set in fireworks history:

- **The largest firework shell ever launched was 4.7 feet (1.4 m) wide and weighed 2,797 pounds (1,269 kg). It contained 380 individual comets. The mortar needed to launch the shell was over 5 feet (1.6 m) long. The firework was successfully fired on February 8, 2020, in Colorado.**
- **A Catherine wheel (sometimes also called a pinwheel) is a firework consisting of small, rocketlike fireworks placed around the rim of a cardboard or wood disk. When ignited, the wheel spins rapidly, throwing off showers of sparks. A typical Catherine wheel available to consumers may be about 8 to 18 inches (20 to 45 cm) wide. The largest Catherine wheel ever made was produced in the tiny Mediterranean island nation of Malta. Built by the Lily Fireworks Factory, the Catherine wheel was 105 feet (32 m) in diameter. Technicians lit the wheel on June 18, 2011. The power from the explosion was enough to make the wheel complete four entire revolutions.**
- **The largest firework display in the world was held in the Philippines on January 1, 2016. Over 810,000 fireworks were shot off in just over one hour.**

firework. For instance, the workers in one building may make nothing but one type of fountain while those in another building make nothing but firecrackers. Only a small number of people are allowed to work in each building to keep the damage from any accident contained to as small an area as possible and reduce injuries.

Accidents

As we've discussed, fireworks are not only dangerous to handle but dangerous to manufacture. Workers must take enormous care when handling materials that are potentially highly flammable and explosive. For example, they work with large quantities of black powder, potassium perchlorate, and other dangerous materials, which increases the amount of danger if all of them were to be accidentally set off.

In 2000 a fireworks factory in the Netherlands blew up. Nearly two thousand buildings and homes were destroyed or damaged, 950 people were injured, and 23 were killed. One of the worst fireworks factory accidents occurred in Indonesia in 2017 and killed 49 people. In 2024 an explosion at a fireworks factory in Thailand killed more than 20 people. That year a fire in a factory in India also killed 11 people and injured about 150 others.

Many of these accidents took place in countries where there is little official oversight and few regulations for fireworks. In Mexico, for example, where fireworks are very popular, there are hundreds of small manufacturing shops set up by families in their homes, often without proper training or safety precautions. In and around Tultepec, a city in Mexico, there are more than five hundred of these types of fireworks shops. A 2014 survey in India showed that nearly 97 percent of workers in fireworks factories received little or no safety training, safe tools, or protective clothing.

Most accidents occur when fireworks are made illegally.

Other countries, such as England, Germany, Japan, and the United States, have stricter rules and laws regulating how fireworks are manufactured. But accidents still happen. One of the earliest disasters in the United States occurred in 1869 when a fireworks factory in Petersburg, Virginia, exploded, killing twelve workers. But most accidents occur when fireworks are made illegally. In 1983 an illegal fireworks factory in Tennessee blew up, killing eleven people. The explosion could be heard up to 20 miles (32 km) away.

Chapter 4

Professional and Consumer Fireworks

The Bureau of Alcohol, Tobacco, Firearms and Explosives (ATF), the US agency assigned with overseeing and regulating the use of explosives, defines display fireworks as large fireworks used in shows, generally under the supervision of a trained pyrotechnician. Only trained pyrotechnicians should handle several other types of pyrotechnics, such as indoor fireworks. Consumer fireworks, on the other hand, are defined as small fireworks. Most adults can buy and safely use these. They are usually sold at stands, typically around the Fourth of July holiday. They include ground devices such as fountains and noisemakers containing less than 0.0018 ounces (50 mg) of flash powder, and aerial devices, such as skyrockets, containing less than 0.0046 ounces (130 mg) of flash powder. The ATF defines flash powder as any composition that creates a flash and noise when ignited, including black powder. Because consumer fireworks contain pyrotechnic compositions classified by ATF as explosive materials, the manufacturing of consumer fireworks for commercial purposes requires a special license from the ATF.

Some US fireworks stands are open year-round, and others are only open in the summer, leading up to the Fourth of July. Both types of retailers tend to make most of their yearly revenue around this holiday because celebrating it with fireworks is so popular.

Most states regulate the sale of fireworks, but even so, the US industry earns more than $400 million every year from selling display fireworks and more than $2 billion from consumer fireworks.

One of the first companies organized to import and sell consumer fireworks across the United States was Black Cat Fireworks. Li & Fung, a Chinese company operating out of Hong Kong, originated the Black Cat brand. It opened for business in the United States in the 1940s. In 1952 it registered its name as a trademark, making it the oldest registered brand of fireworks in the country. Black Cat is also one of the largest manufacturers of fireworks in the United Kingdom.

Today several large companies in the United States import and distribute consumer fireworks. Winco Fireworks, for instance, distributes Black Cat fireworks to retailers across the United States. People can find their stands in parking lots for malls and shopping centers across the country in the weeks leading up to the Fourth of July. Similarly, people can spot temporary sales tents for Phantom Fireworks, one of the largest of the companies specializing in fireworks, in the weeks prior to the Fourth of July.

Phantom Fireworks

The largest dealer in consumer fireworks in the United States is Phantom Fireworks. Currently based on a 17-acre (6.9 ha) campus near Youngstown, Ohio, the company was founded in the early 1970s by Bruce J. Zoldan. It began doing business as Phantom Fireworks in 1977. It currently operates a chain of eighty fireworks stores that are open all year in fifteen states, and it supplies retailers in forty-seven states at specific times during the year. While the company largely imports its fireworks from China, Phantom acquired the Diamond Sparkler Manufacturing Company in 1985. At the time, Diamond Sparkler was the only company in the United States that created sparklers, creating up to eight hundred thousand sparklers every day.

Phantom also operates nearly two thousand temporary stands across the US around the Fourth of July. The company also distributes fireworks manufactured by other leading companies such as Grucci (see pages 26–27).

Phantom Fireworks has long been active in promoting safety in both the manufacture and use of fireworks. It participates in the American Fireworks Standards Laboratory, an independent organization that the fireworks industry created to set standards for fireworks safety and test products for compliance with its rules. Established in 1989, the laboratory has tested more than one hundred million cases of consumer fireworks. Phantom is also a leading member of national organizations such as the American Pyrotechnics Association, the National Fireworks Association, and the Pyrotechnics Guild International (PGI), all of which are devoted to the safe manufacture and use of fireworks.

Indoor Fireworks

Using fireworks inside a building or room might sound like the very last thing anyone would want to do. But some fireworks are specially designed for indoors. Most of these fireworks still produce heat, so they need to be used very carefully—they should not be used anywhere near any flammable materials, for instance. But they are made from chemicals that are not harmful if used in an enclosed space. For example, in some fireworks, the sparks are not only cool to the touch, but there is no smoke or smell. So spark machines are popular for events such as concerts, parties, or weddings where people—either performers or the audience—may be near the machines. What are some other examples of indoor fireworks?

Ice Fountains

Ice fountains are small, tube-shaped fireworks that produce a jet of bright sparks. They are called ice fountains because the sparks from the fountain are not hot. They are sometimes called cake fountains because they can be inserted into the top of a birthday cake instead of a candle.

Flame Projectors

Flame projectors do just what their name suggests: They shoot a bright jet of flame straight into the air. The difference between a flame projector and an ice fountain is that the flame from the projector lasts for only a second or two. Flame projectors are very popular at rock concerts. Some flame projectors are fueled by propane so they can be precisely controlled by an operator. The operator adjusts the valve to control how much propane is released.

Spark Machines

A spark machine produces a fountain of bright sparks by heating titanium or zirconium powder until the granules are glowing white. The machine then cools the granules until they are at a safe temperature but continue to glow. These granules, or sparks, release from a vent at the top of the machine. The visual effect is the same as a traditional fireworks fountain but is much safer.

Harmless sparks generated by special machines create a spectacular effect for concerts, weddings, and other events.

Pyrotechnic Look-Alikes

The next two categories are not strictly pyrotechnics—since there is no heat, fire, or explosives involved—but the effects can be very similar to traditional fireworks, and many professional pyrotechnicians include them in their repertoire.

Glitter, Confetti, and Streamer Launchers

Compressed air or carbon dioxide is used to fire cartridges filled with glitter, confetti, or streamers from a gunlike device either straight up into the air or over the heads of an audience. The effect can sometimes look just like a traditional firework.

Smoke and Fog

Using dry ice or special fluids, machines can create smoke and fog. Some fog machines add warm water to dry ice, creating a cold, low-lying fog. This can create a spooky effect for Halloween. Other fog machines use mineral oil or a mixture of water and glycerin called fog juice to create clouds of "smoke." The fluid heats up inside the machine and

Becoming a Pyrotechnician

Each state has its own rules regarding pyrotechnics, but they are all more or less similar. Most states have fire prevention laws that prohibit anyone from designing, setting up, or conducting a fireworks display unless that person is certified as a pyrotechnician by both state and federal authorities. At least one certified pyrotechnician is usually required to be on the site where the fireworks display is being set up and conducted. Motion picture special effects artists who handle pyrotechnics also need to be certified and licensed.

To obtain a pyrotechnician's license, you need to take an active part in a certain number of fireworks shows over a set time. The number of shows and length of time depends on your state, but typically you can complete the requirements as a volunteer. This experience can be with a professional pyrotechnician, through a pyrotechnics manufacturer or distributor, or with a pyrotechnics club. There are several regional clubs around the country, such as the Bluegrass Pyrotechnics Guild, the Heartland Pyrotechnic Arts Association, and the Mid-Atlantic Pyrotechnic Arts Guild (see more on page 99).

Once you have accumulated the necessary experience, you will take a written test. If you pass, you will be issued a license by your state's fire marshal. This license only allows you to shoot off display fireworks. To purchase and store them, you need a special permit from the ATF.

blows out through a nozzle. Machines called Cryo-Jets use liquid nitrogen to create masses of dense white clouds. Unlike smoke, which is warm and rises into the air, the fog created by dry ice and nitrogen is very cold and flows down, often forming a deep blanket of fog on the ground or floor.

Consumer Fireworks

There may seem to be a dazzling variety of different consumer fireworks available, but there are only a handful of basic types. Let's go through a few of them.

Sparklers

The simplest type of firework is a sparkler. It's a heavy metal wire typically about 1 foot (30 cm) long and up to 3 feet (1 m). A mixture made up of a pyrotechnic compound and powdered metal coats one end of the metal wire. Powdered metals come in different types. The type of powdered metal determines the color of the sparks. As the compound burns, it heats the metal, creating a shower of bright sparks.

Although sparklers are among the simplest of fireworks and are generally safe, like any firework, they can be dangerous. The main danger comes from a sparkler's heat. As the pyrotechnic compound burns, it can heat the wire to a temperature of 1,800°F to 3,000°F (980°C to 1,650°C)—hot enough to cause severe burns to human skin or damage to property.

Firecrackers

The firecracker is probably the most iconic of all consumer fireworks and has been around the longest. In its simplest form, it is a small amount of black powder wrapped tightly in a paper tube. Governments heavily regulate firecrackers since they're explosive.

Skyrockets

Skyrockets are the second most recognized types of fireworks. A large skyrocket can reach heights of hundreds of feet in the air before bursting. Bottle rockets are miniature skyrockets, only 1 inch (2.5 cm) or so long, attached to a slender wooden stick. They get their name because the stick is usually placed in the neck of a soft drink bottle. At the end of their flight, they explode with a sharp bang.

Fountains

Fountains come in all sizes. They usually resemble cones, tubes, or wide, cake-shaped cylinders. As their name suggests, they create beautiful fountains of colored sparks, usually without any loud noises.

Roman Candles

The Roman candle is another popular firework that has been around for centuries. It is a long tube. One end of the tube is stuck in the ground or into some sort of support. When ignited, the Roman candle shoots a series of bright, flaming balls.

Catherine Wheels

A Catherine wheel is essentially several small rocketlike devices—called drivers—mounted on the rim of a cardboard disk. The disk can be fastened to a post by driving a nail through the center of the disk. When lit, the rockets spin the disk rapidly like a car tire, creating a circular spray of bright sparks. The firework gets its name from Saint Catherine, who, legend says, was sacrificed on a wheel.

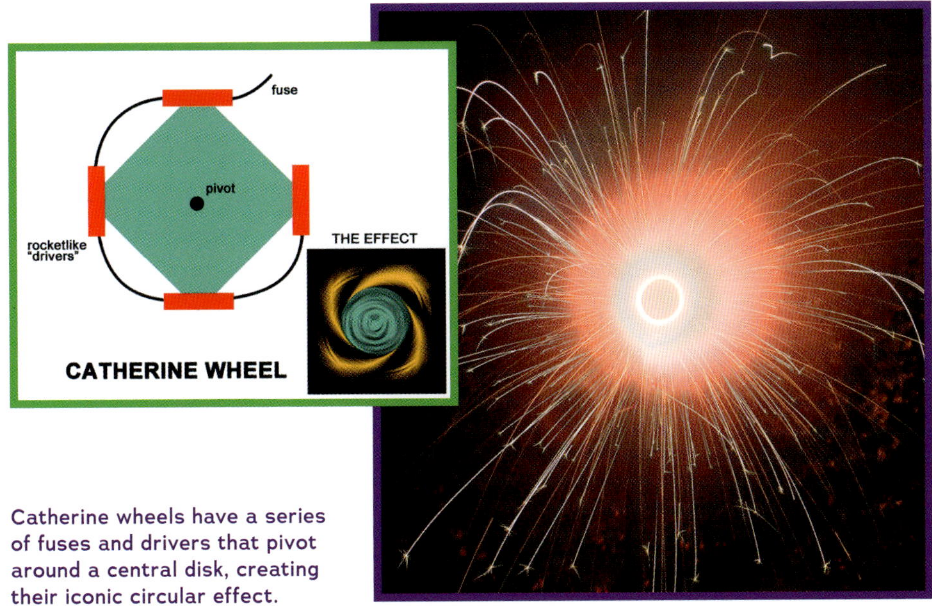

Catherine wheels have a series of fuses and drivers that pivot around a central disk, creating their iconic circular effect.

Ground spinners are related to the Catherine wheel, but these are placed on the ground. When lit, ground spinners shoot off sparks and make crackling sounds as they spin rapidly.

Cakes, or Barrages

A cake, or barrage, is a cluster of small tubes. Each tube is a firework. Some may produce a shower or jet of sparks like a fountain. Other tubes may launch effects into the air. Some barrages may be a cluster of similar effects, each one alike, while others may change effects as each tube ignites. These effects may be flashes of light or colors, bangs or crackling sounds, or sparkles. They are among the most popular types of fireworks because of their variety and their ability to burn for up to one to two minutes, longer than the typical solo firework.

Smoke Bombs and Snakes

Smoke bombs do exactly what their name suggests: When lit, they produce dense clouds of smoke, often colored. Snakes are probably one of the most unusual fireworks. They look like small black pellets or cones. When lit they don't produce sparks or flashes or noise. Instead, they uncoil into long, snakelike shapes of ash.

US Firework Regulation

In the United States, the Consumer Product Safety Commission has strict rules governing how fireworks are made, packaged, and labeled. The commission collects samples of fireworks directly from dealers and manufacturers. It then takes these samples to a laboratory where they are tested for safety. Handlers check labels for accuracy and to make sure they include all legally required information such as a caution warning. If a firework fails any of these tests, it is considered a hazardous substance and is banned from sale.

One of the tests fireworks must undergo is checking the amount of combustible pyrotechnic material—such as black powder or flash powder—they contain. Firecrackers and other ground fireworks can only

Fireworks and the Law

People can easily mishandle fireworks, so they are strictly regulated in many places. In 1731 Rhode Island lawmakers passed a law to prevent the "mischievous use of pyrotechnics," due to pranks involving firecrackers getting out of hand. By the early 1900s, fireworks—particularly the firecracker—became so pervasive, annoying, and dangerous that in 1907 a New York physician named Julia Barnett Rice formed the Society for the Suppression of Unnecessary Noise, which lobbied for laws to restrict the sale and use of fireworks of all kinds. She even received the endorsement of famed author Mark Twain. With his support, she was able to get laws passed nationwide.

Massachusetts is the only state in the US that bans the private sale of fireworks outright, even though the state was the first to recognize the Fourth of July as a state holiday. Eighteen states only permit users to use fireworks that do not launch into the air and do not explode. As such, fireworks such as fountains, sparklers, and pinwheels are the only permitted types under these laws. Most other states allow the purchase and use of skyrockets and fountains. Eighteen states ban firecrackers, and all states put some limit on the time of day that people can set off fireworks to keep fireworks from becoming a nuisance. During dry conditions, such as when there is danger of wildfires, the use of fireworks might be temporarily banned. Many county and city regulations supersede the state laws by further limiting or even entirely banning the use of pyrotechnics, or fireworks. For example, some counties in California are especially susceptible to fires, and most types of fireworks are banned in those areas.

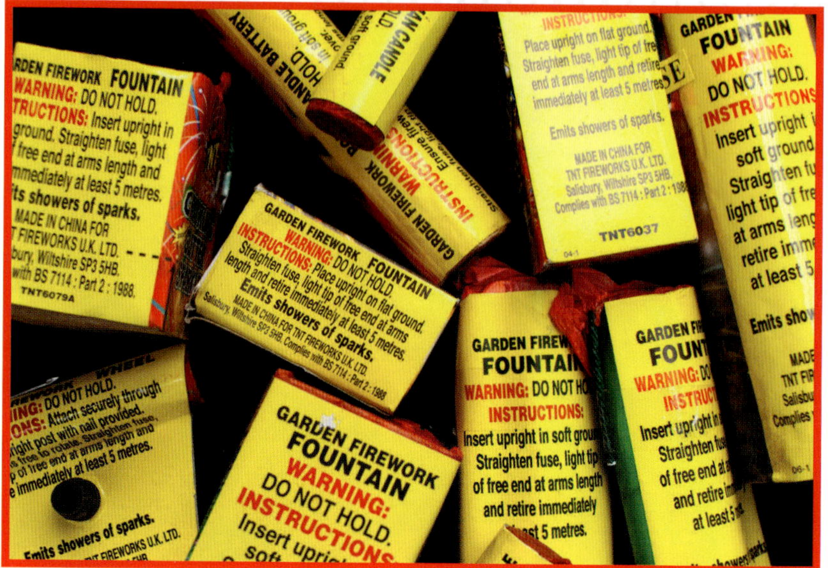

Firework packages feature cautionary messages specific to the type of firework and directions for how to handle and light them. For example, a fountain, Roman candle, or other ground or aerial firework will often warn users not to hold it during and after ignition. But sparklers tell users how to safely hold the sparkler while it's lit.

contain 50 mg (0.0018 ounces) of powder. Aerial fireworks, designed to explode in the air, can only contain up to 130 mg (0.0053 ounces) of powder.

Other tests include the following:

- Testing that fuses burn for no less than three and no more than nine seconds
- Testing that fireworks have sturdy bases that prevent them from tipping over
- Testing a firework's packaging so no powder can leak out
- Testing for any of the following potentially hazardous ingredients: arsenic sulfide, arsenates, arsenites, boron, chlorates, gallates, gallic acid, magnesium, mercury salts, phosphorous, picrates, picric acid, thiocyanates, titanium, or zirconium. No fireworks are allowed to have any of these ingredients.
- Inspecting the length and diameter of mortar tubes, as well as the sticks on bottle rockets

The Consumer Product Safety Commission requires all labels on fireworks to contain the word CAUTION or WARNING. They must contain a description of the effect and potential hazards, such as "shoots flaming balls" or "emits sparks," and a description of how the firework is to be handled safely. Each type of firework has a different required label. A typical warning label for a fountain will read:

WARNING
EMITS SHOWERS OF SPARKS.
Use only under adult supervision.
For outdoor use only.
Place on level surface.
Light fuse and get away.

A sparkler's warning label will typically read:

CAUTION
Use only under adult supervision.
For outdoor use only.
Do not touch glowing wire.
Hold in hand with arm extended away from body.
Keep burning end or sparks away from apparel or other flammable material.

Fireworks Regulation Around the World

While fireworks are legal in most countries around the world, they are strictly regulated and even banned in others. Most of the countries that do permit fireworks limit their sale and use to certain holidays. Fireworks in Germany, for instance, can only be sold during the three days before New Year's Eve, and only adults can purchase them. Finland has similar restrictions, banning the sale of fireworks except on New Year's Eve and New Year's Day. Even then, they can only be set off between 6 p.m. and 2 a.m. on New Year's Eve, and anybody who uses

Fireworks Etiquette

Many people enjoy having a private fireworks display in their own backyard on the Fourth of July. Aside from safety concerns (see page 36), being considerate for your neighbors is an important part of having fun with fireworks.

The first thing you should check is whether it is legal to shoot off fireworks in your backyard. Your local police department will let you know if it is all right or if there are any restrictions on the types of fireworks you can use.

Many fireworks are noisy. If you have pets, make sure they are secured in a safe location, so they cannot run away if the noise upsets them. Check in with your neighbors to see if they are okay with sharp, loud noises, especially from fireworks such as firecrackers. They can sound like gunfire, which might upset some people.

Be aware of the size of the fireworks you plan to use. If the space is small, such as a cramped backyard, you don't want to shoot off fireworks that might infringe on someone else's property . . . or even perhaps endanger their home. Keeping at least 150 feet (45 m) from other houses is a good rule of thumb. If your yard is small, ground-based effects such as fountains might be a better idea than fireworks that shoot high into the air.

Plan the time for shooting off your fireworks. Don't do it too early in the morning or too late at night.

Clean up afterward. Fireworks are naturally messy. You may find shreds of paper not only all over your own yard but in your neighbors' yards as well.

fireworks is required to wear safety goggles. The laws in Ireland are even stricter. The sale of fireworks is fully restricted and anyone using fireworks is required to have a professional fireworks operator present.

While France has no national ban on fireworks, many cities such as Paris and Strasbourg consider fireworks a fire hazard and have their own ban on them. In Sweden, only citizens over the age of eighteen are permitted to purchase fireworks, and both a permit and special training are required to launch rockets with sticks. Chile has banned most people from using fireworks entirely. No one can buy or use them without a license.

Some cities, states, and countries are more concerned with the environmental effect of fireworks than with their safety issues. Firecrackers are so popular in India that the city of Delhi banned fireworks in 2017 due to concerns about air pollution. This was largely due to dangerous elements such as barium, which is toxic, being an ingredient in fireworks. In 2023 the Supreme Court of India expanded the ban on fireworks containing barium and other dangerous chemicals to the entire country.

Trained pyrotechnicians take safety precautions as they set up 2.6 tons (2.4 t) of fireworks along the ramparts of Edinburgh Castle in Scotland.

Chapter 5

Practical Fireworks

Fireworks aren't always meant to entertain or look pretty. They can also have a very practical purpose. Rockets, in fact, have saved thousands of lives. What types of practical pyrotechnics are there?

Kitchen Matches

The most familiar form of pyrotechnics is one that most people might be surprised by: the ordinary kitchen match. John Walker, a British pharmacist, created the first matches in 1826. He had been working on developing a new pastelike type of black powder. After stirring a mixture of chemicals with a wood stick, he scraped the stick against the rough brick of his fireplace hearth to clean it . . . and the stick burst into flame. He soon began selling what he called friction lights at his drugstore. His first matches were made of strips of cardboard with a dry coating of chemicals on one end, but he soon began using slivers of wood. He sold these new matches in small boxes equipped with a strip of sandpaper for striking.

Walker's matches were an immediate success with the public. But because he failed to get a patent—the legal right to exclude others

Swallow brand matches were produced by Swedish Match Industries AB, which has been a leading match manufacturer for over 150 years. Companies would add their own beautifully designed labels. Matchbox labels are still popular collector's items.

from making, using, or selling a piece of work—on his invention, others quickly copied his idea.

Until Walker created matches, starting a fire was often tiresome, time-consuming, and haphazard, and typically required striking a piece of flint with a steel tool to get a spark. Walker's invention allowed anyone to create fire almost instantly anywhere with little effort.

But Walker's matches posed some danger. Since any amount of friction might set one off, people were worried about carrying or storing them. Swedish inventors Gustaf Erik Pasch and Johan Edvard Lundström solved this problem in 1844 by separating two of the ingredients of the coating, leaving one on the head of the match and placing the other on the striking surface. The match could not ignite until someone struck it on the striking surface. These matches became known as safety matches, and with their familiar red heads, they are virtually identical in appearance to the kitchen matches still used.

Philadelphia, Pennsylvania, attorney Joshua Pusey, who liked to smoke cigars, grew tired of having to carry a box of wooden matches everywhere he went. To solve this problem, he created matches from slivers of paper. Then he took another piece of small paper, folded it in half, and added a coarse striking surface to the exterior. This same piece of folded paper also became a container to hold the matches. Patented in 1892, this was the birth of the modern matchbook. It spread everywhere in the United States. Even when small butane (liquid gas) lighters became popular, Americans continued to use matches. On average, Americans strike five hundred billion matches every year.

Signal Rockets

On April 10, 1912, the largest passenger ship in the world, the *Titanic*, began its first voyage across the Atlantic. Five days later, it sank after colliding with an iceberg.

Although the ship was equipped with a radio, it had been busy receiving and sending personal messages to and from passengers. Perhaps that is why crew members and the captain either ignored or failed to take action in response to warnings of nearby ice. The ship struck an iceberg at 11:40 p.m.

The *Titanic* carried thirty-six signal rockets. They were designed to explode several hundred feet above the ship, making a loud bang, followed by a shower of bright, white sparks. By international agreement, a series of these rockets fired at one-minute intervals would alert any nearby ship that help was immediately needed. At 12:45 a.m., an officer of the *Titanic* fired one rocket. Over the next hour, the crew fired another seven—but not at the agreed-upon one-minute intervals that would have signaled disaster. Instead, the rockets were fired anywhere from seven to eight minutes apart. If a passing ship were to have seen these signals, they would have interpreted these signals to mean, "Here is my position, having a navigation problem, please keep clear." That's almost exactly the opposite of what the *Titanic* needed. Instead of rushing to the *Titanic*'s rescue, the few ships that saw the rockets stayed clear.

One result of the *Titanic*'s tragic sinking was the creation of the International Convention for the Safety of Life at Sea, an international

A lifesaving rocket in its launcher. It was designed to carry a line from the shore to a ship in distress.

maritime treaty that sets safety standards for merchant vessels. According to its regulations, ships are required to carry at least twelve signal rockets, as well as an additional four in each lifeboat. Each lifeboat is equipped with instructions on how to use the signal rockets.

One of the leading producers of signal rockets is Comet. German engineer Friedrich Wilhelm Sander founded the company in the 1930s. Sander was an enthusiastic proponent of using rockets to propel vehicles. It was Sander's rockets, for instance, that powered the first rocket-propelled aircraft in 1928. Today, the company manufactures line-carrying rockets, flares, and smoke signals that navies and merchant ships all over the world use.

Lifesaving Rockets

Most shipwrecks occur close to shore due to shallow water or hidden reefs. When a captain steers a ship too close to either of these, the ship can run aground, or get stuck. Many ships become stranded this way.

In 1807 British inventor Henry Trengrouse proposed using rockets to carry lines, or ropes, to stranded ships. The idea was that a rocket could carry a light line or rope from the shore to the ship. The crew would use this line to pull in a heavier rope, which would be tied to the end of the light line and could then be used as a pulley system to transfer crew and passengers to safety. But as good as this idea was, scientists hadn't developed rockets enough for them to be up to the task. Rockets didn't have enough range, which was typically less than 1 mile (1.6 km), to span the distance between a stranded ship and its rescuers. In 1865 Edward Mounier Boxer, a colonel of the British Royal Laboratory of the Royal Arsenal, developed rockets powerful and accurate enough to be used as line carriers. His two-stage rocket had two rockets mounted tip to end. Once the first rocket had burned out, the second rocket ignited automatically, adding its speed to that of the first one. The rocket could carry a line up to 1,500 to 2,100 feet (457 to 640 m).

In the 1880s, William Schermuly and his son, Captain Conrad Schermuly, began working on a new line-carrying rocket. They were concerned about the many lives still being lost within sight of land. So, they developed a rocket system that would be lighter and more accurate than the earlier systems that the Royal Laboratory invented. The rocket would carry a light line from ship to shore or from ship to ship. This would allow the crew to pull in a heavier cable attached to the light line. They finished the development of their line-throwing rocket in 1897. The rocket looked like a pistol with a large cylindrical barrel, which held the rocket. The device was heavy and large enough that a tripod was often needed to support it. One of the Schermulys' most important innovations for the rocket was a special container for the line that allowed it to fly toward the ship smoothly and without tangling. In World War I, soldiers used the Schermulys' line-carrying rockets to carry telegraph wires between trenches.

In 1920 Conrad Schermuly started redesigning the line-carrying rocket. He named it the Pistol Rocket Apparatus and opened Schermuly Pistol Rocket Apparatus in 1926. In 1929 British law required all ships weighing over 500 tons (454 t) to carry the gun.

Once the Schermuly rockets became popular, ships around the world began stocking line-carrying rockets. The shoreline was a much bigger target than a ship stranded in shallow water. Sailors could fire rockets that would penetrate the ground and act as an anchor. The line attached to the rocket could then be used to guide lifeboats safely to shore. For decades, the Schermuly company was a leading manufacturer of line-carrying rockets for stranded ships.

Members of a flood rescue squad, a civil defense organization, and a police rescue squad examine a pistol rocket launcher in the 1960s. Line-carrying rockets continue to be a popular safety tool aboard ships.

Historian Roddam Narasimha of the National Aeronautical Laboratory and Indian Institute of Science estimated that in the British Isles alone, line-carrying rockets saved more than fifteen thousand lives between 1871 and 1962. Today's line-carrying rockets come in compact, portable cases that contain not only the rocket but also over 800 feet (243 m) of line. Being portable, they can be used anywhere: from ship to shore, shore to ship, between ships, or even in rescues on land, where a line might need to extend across a river or ravine.

Flares

Flares, sometimes called fusees, are pyrotechnic devices that create a bright, often colored, light to attract attention or to warn of danger. Handheld flares look like large, thick tubes and are bright enough to be seen in daylight. They are used to signal nearby rescuers to a person's position. Flares can produce a bright red or orange flame that can be seen for miles or a bright white light that can illuminate a small area.

The road flare is probably the most familiar type of flare. It is a red cylinder typically about 1 foot (30 cm) long. It contains flammable materials, which can be ignited by striking one end of the flare in the same way one would light a kitchen match. Many drivers carry one or more of them in their car. If their car breaks down, drivers can use road flares to warn other drivers to watch out for the stranded car. Police, firefighters, and construction crews use road flares as warnings and to mark hazards, such as accidents, stuck vehicles, damage from storms, and more.

A parachute flare is similar in appearance to a handheld flare. But instead of creating a brightly colored flame, it launches a bright red flare into the air. The flare can reach up to 980 feet (300 m) in the sky. Then, for around forty seconds, the burning flare slowly descends on a little parachute. Search and rescue teams in the mountains, sea, or remote areas often use parachute flares.

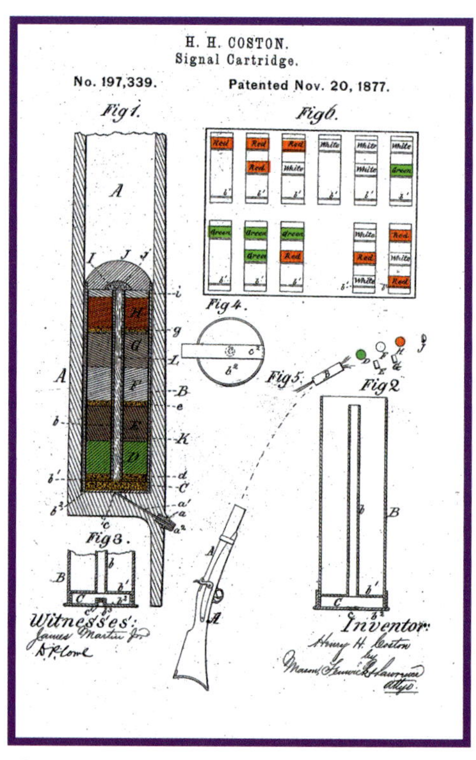

The Coston flare gun could be loaded with different colored cartridges so that, when someone fired the gun, the correct signal was produced in a quick sequence.

An illuminating rocket is another handheld device often used in search and rescue missions. This rocket launches a flare, which is attached to a parachute. It is similar to a parachute flare. But instead of a red flame, it produces a brilliant white light that illuminates a large area of the ground below.

Specially designed handguns can also launch flares. In 1859 American naval officer Benjamin Franklin Coston came up with the idea of the Coston Telegraphic Night Signal, a flare gun. Coston's flare could burn in any desired sequence of multiple colors. This meant it could be used to create signals in a prearranged code. Unfortunately, Coston's official duties prevented him from getting a patent, which made it hard for early manufacturers to access the design for the invention and produce it. Coston also wasn't able to mass-produce and distribute the flares himself at the time. But his wife, Martha, would later finish his work (see page 24).

Nearly two decades later, in 1877, Edward Wilson Very, a lieutenant in the US Navy, patented another flare gun. But where Coston's flare gun was sophisticated and capable of multiple colors, Very's gun could fire only a single flare that burned with one color. Even so, this gun is still widely used. The original Very pistol shot a bright flare—called a Very light—to a height of about 300 feet (90 m) and could be seen for at least 3 miles (5 km). A modern Very pistol can launch a flare about 1,000 feet (300 m) into the air. The flare explodes with a loud bang to attract attention and then burns with a bright red or white light. The flare is often attached to a small parachute to make it descend slowly so it stays visible for as long as possible.

Incendiary Flares

Incendiary flares are made to deliberately start fires. Firefighters will often start controlled fires to clear a forest of dead leaves, tree limbs, and other debris. In creating a controlled burn, they can help prevent an uncontrolled, destructive wildfire that might destroy thousands of acres of land along with people's homes and businesses. Controlled fires can also be used to contain ongoing wildfires and forest fires. Firefighters burn debris such as dead wood and leaves that would provide fuel for the larger fire.

Firefighters and forest management personnel use specially made incendiary flares that burn at temperatures up to 4,000°F (2,200°C) and will even burn underwater. The flares are designed so people can launch them from guns that resemble Very pistols or throw them by hand. These devices are only available to trained professional firefighters.

Smoke Signals

Smoke signals are pyrotechnic devices designed to produce smoke. These come in all sizes, from small buckets to handheld signals. They produce billows of smoke in different colors, often orange since it is an unnatural color for smoke and easily attracts attention. Orange is also an international signal for distress. One type of handheld smoke signal is designed for life rafts or lifeboats. It produces a red flare at one end and orange smoke from the other. Other smoke signals are designed to float on water as they operate. These smoke signals are required on merchant ships, and people can use them to mark the position of a crew member who has fallen overboard.

Flash-Bangs

Also known as stun bombs, flash-bangs are small, nonlethal explosive devices that law enforcement and the military use in combat and riot control. They create a blinding flash of light along with a sharp, extremely loud bang about a thousand times louder than a jet engine. The combination of light and sound can stun anyone standing nearby, temporarily confusing or disorienting them.

Airbags

Another lifesaving device that depends on pyrotechnics is the airbag. Airbags have been standard in cars since the late 1990s. When a sensor in the engine compartment detects a collision, a signal is sent to an inflator inside a strong nylon bag, which is kept folded. The signal triggers a very small explosive device, which releases a large amount of harmless nitrogen gas that inflates the bag in twenty to thirty milliseconds.

From Stage to Movies

Before they appeared in movies, pyrotechnic effects were used onstage. Some of the earliest appearances of pyrotechnics were in mystery plays. Often put on by a church, mystery plays were based on biblical stories or the lives of saints. In 1379 a mystery play in Vicenza, Italy, incorporated the appearance of doves after a bright flash of light and a

Pyrotechnics can create highly realistic effects, such as this simulated car explosion that was created for the German television show *Der Bozen Krimi*.

loud bang. Other mystery plays might have used effects such as smoke or a shower of sparks to announce the appearance of saints or angels.

By the 1700s, stage technicians used fireworks to create effects such as lightning, thunder, volcanoes, and earthquakes. One invention that is still used in modern motion picture special effects is the squib. This device resembles a small firecracker and can be used to create many different effects. Some squibs are made to burn slowly, while others might explode like the firecracker they resemble. Originally, people used squibs to create flashes of light, clouds of smoke, or sharp bangs that might indicate storms, gunfire, or the appearance of devils or demons. But in modern motion pictures, special effects technicians use squibs—which are now fired electronically—to duplicate sounds or visuals such as a bullet hitting something.

Following the introduction of fireworks to the stage, people added more pyrotechnic effects such as flash paper and flash powder. Flash paper is a sheet of thin paper treated with nitric acid. When ignited by even as little as a spark, it disappears almost instantly in a burst of bright flame. Flash powder contains magnesium or aluminum powder, which burns with an intensely white flash of light. Both of these have been staples of stage magicians for more than a century. For instance, a magician might use flash paper to create a flash of flame from their fingertips. A magician can use flash powder to create a brief burst of bright light and a cloud of smoke to distract the audience when they want something to seemingly disappear or reappear.

Pyrotechnic effects made the transition from stage to screen as early as the end of the 1800s. The earliest motion pictures were often little more than stage productions recorded on film. Later, many of the same special effects used in stage productions were also used in motion pictures. One of the first masters of special effects in movies, Georges Méliès (1861–1938), had been a professional magician before making movies. He brought his knowledge of stage pyrotechnic effects—such as smoke bombs and flash powder—and incorporated it into his films.

Pyrotechnic effects aren't limited to plays, movies, and magic. In the 1960s, rock musicians, such as Led Zeppelin and Alice Cooper, added pyrotechnic effects including smoke bombs and flash powder to their performances. By the 1980s, Van Halen, Paul McCartney, and AC/DC were regularly enhancing their stage shows with fireworks. In 2024 artists such as Beyoncé and Lady Gaga included pyrotechnic effects that rival those of the Fourth of July in their shows.

Types of Movie Pyrotechnics

Movie pyrotechnics can be divided into four main classes:

- **Open flame.** Fireplaces, lava flows, candles, forest fires, volcanoes, some bombs
- **Sparks.** Electrical failures, Frankenstein labs
- **Smoke.** Outdoor fires, chimneys, cigars and cigarettes, auto exhaust, firearm simulation, smoke following explosions
- **Explosions.** Bullet and artillery hits, bombs, firearm simulation

Open flame fire effects are often used to imitate everything from bombs exploding in war movies to volcanoes. For instance, a huge

A car appears to be flipped over by an explosion in this exciting scene that expert pyrotechnicians created for a motion picture.

ball of flame will be created if a technician launches a container of flammable liquid into the air using compressed gas, propane, or an explosive device. The flammable fluid spreads into a fine mist and is ignited by the burning powder that launched it. The result is a ball of flame that looks like an explosion much larger than it really is. This method was used to create a realistic nuclear explosion in the 2023 film *Oppenheimer* (see page 71). Technicians might add chunks of sponge or foam to give the effect of the explosion causing rocks and other debris to fly into the air.

Sparks are often used when some kind of electrical effect is needed, such as a short circuit in an electrical appliance. Sparks can also create the effect of a bullet ricocheting from a rock or metal surface. Sometimes a technician might use a firework as simple as an ordinary sparkler to create sparks and even to imitate the sparks flying off welding equipment.

The Lydecker Brothers

After Méliès pioneered the field of special effects in movie productions, brothers Howard and Theodore Lydecker became the film industry standard of movie pyrotechnician masters. Their father, Howard C. Lydecker, had created motion picture special effects using miniatures, something Howard and Theodore turned into a fine art. A miniature is a scale model of a building, ship, aircraft, or car that is typically much smaller than the real thing. The use of miniatures is a cost-saving technique. For instance, a script might call for a building to explode. Instead of destroying an entire building, which would be both very expensive and very dangerous, a small, realistic model is made. The model can then be blown up safely and at little cost. If filmed carefully and at just the right angle, the exploding model will look like the real thing to an audience.

In addition to creating realistic model buildings, ships, and aircraft, the Lydecker brothers also invented ways to blow them up that appeared equally realistic. When directors filmed these explosions in slow motion, the results looked convincing—so realistic that when the Lydecker brothers' effects for the 1942 film *Flying Tigers* were nominated for an Academy Award for best visual effects, Academy officials rejected their nomination because they believed that what they saw on film was real.

The Lydecker brothers kept detailed notebooks describing all the various mixtures of different chemicals they used to create different types of explosions. Some mixtures might make a realistic explosion in water, while others might be perfect for duplicating the appearance of a large building blowing up. In the 1953 movie *Fair Wind to Java*, the brothers made audiences believe an entire island had blown up when they re-created the 1883 eruption of the volcano Krakatoa in Indonesia.

The work of the Lydecker brothers inspired later masters of motion picture special effects, such as Joe Viskocil, who created memorable pyrotechnic effects such as the explosion of the Death Star in the 1977 film *Star Wars*. Many techniques the brothers developed are still in use.

Smoke can enhance the effect of a fire or imitate fog or clouds. A pyrotechnic device, a "smoke bomb" similar to the ones used as emergency signals, or a smoke machine might create the smoke. Smoke machines create smoke by internally spraying a fine mist of oily liquid over a hot surface. The hot oil then emerges as a dense cloud of smoke.

Explosions can re-create many effects such as bombs and bullet hits, which use squibs that are not very different from those used in mystery plays. The simplest squib consists of two wires joined by a small segment of Nichrome wire. This is a kind of metal that heats up when an electric charge passes through it. The wire is coated with a pyrotechnic material and then sealed. When a current passes through the Nichrome wire, it heats up and ignites the material. (The wires inside a toaster are also made of Nichrome. You can see them heat up when you turn the toaster on.)

Technicians often ignite squibs remotely. Once ignited, an electric charge will pass through the squib. The squib then produces a small explosion with smoke, sparks, or a burst of dust or debris, depending on the effect desired. To achieve the effect of the rapid impact of a machine gun's bullets, technicians will quickly ignite a row of squibs.

Miniatures in Movies

When creating explosions, technicians must keep everybody's safety in mind. One trick technicians use to get around the danger of big explosions is to make a small explosion look much larger than it really is. Another trick is to use a miniature. Miniatures are carefully constructed using pre-weakened materials, meaning they're made in a way that allows the miniature to break apart easily. Because the miniature is much smaller than the actual object, special effects experts require a smaller amount of explosive to create the effect of the object being destroyed. The smaller size and the pre-weakening mean that the model will come apart in a predictable way to keep people safe. A model might also contain special substances that create flame, smoke, sparks, clouds of dust, or other effects to enhance the final

Low Explosives vs. High Explosives

Black powder on its own is considered a low explosive, meaning it burns instead of exploding. A spoonful of black powder will simply burn very quickly when ignited. This kind of rapid burning is called deflagration. It is only when black powder is confined in a container, such as in the cardboard tube of a firecracker, that it will explode.

A highly explosive material such as dynamite will explode regardless of whether it is in a container. Most high explosives aren't ignited by a flame, as black powder is. Instead, people use a small explosive device called a detonator to create a shock that sets off the explosion.

result. Camera operators film the explosion with a high-speed camera. On the movie screen, the scene will appear in slow motion. The slower the explosion appears on-screen, the larger it will seem. An explosion that might have destroyed a miniature in a split second might appear to take several seconds on-screen.

From using miniatures to lowering the number of explosives necessary, technicians go through many steps to re-create the most satisfying appearance of a full-size explosion in the safest way possible.

Making Small Explosions Look Big

Special effects experts most often use black powder to create explosions for movies. Because black powder is considered a low explosive, it is easy for technicians to predict and manipulate its effects. By itself, black powder will simply burn very quickly. But packed into a container, black powder will explode forcefully. The tighter it is packed, the more pressure there is inside the container and the more violent the explosion will be. By controlling how the powder is packed, a special effects artist can determine the final effect and appearance of the explosion.

Technicians go through many steps to re-create the most satisfying appearance of a full-size explosion in the safest way possible.

Normally, black powder burns in a flash, producing white smoke. So special effects artists often add different chemicals to the black powder to create different-colored explosions and smoke. This is the same approach pyrotechnicians employ with creating different colors for a fireworks display.

What are some examples of black powder used on film sets? Directors might want to shoot an explosion for a war movie, so the pyrotechnician digs a hole where the director wants the explosion to occur. The pyrotechnician inserts a mortar into the hole.

Equipment Setup for a Black Powder-Based Ground Explosion

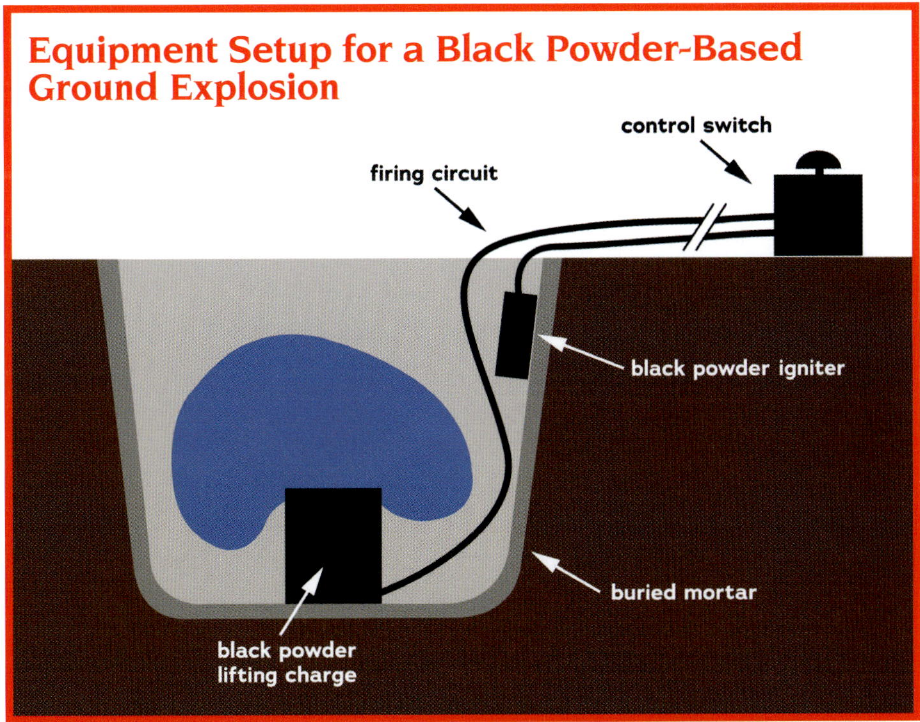

A predetermined "charge weight" of black powder is encased in soft material. The charge weight is the amount of explosive charge needed to create the desired effect. The technician then connects an igniter to the firing circuit. After that, a set designer might add soft materials on top of the charge weight, such as cork, balsa wood, or Styrofoam, to impersonate rocks, dust, and debris when the explosive detonates. These soft materials pose little danger to actors. A technician may also include a fine powder that when thrown into the air by the explosion will create a dense, dark cloud to mimic the cloud of smoke and dust that would result from an actual, full-scale explosion.

A cylindrical mortar will throw dust and debris straight up into the air. A mortar with sloping sides will create an explosion that spreads out, throwing material over a wide area.

If the explosion is supposed to be fiery, technicians will place a bag of flammable liquid over the black powder charge. When the technician ignites the black powder, the explosion throws up a fine spray of the liquid. A split second later, technicians will set off a smaller charge of black powder, which ignites the flammable liquid, blasting a ball of fire into the air and re-creating the appearance of a wartime explosion. In the 1996 movie, *Independence Day*, an alien spaceship blows up the White House. Viskocil placed forty explosive devices in strategic places inside a large model of the building. As the explosives demolished the structure, other devices added smoke, balls of flame, and more.

Other times, a director might want to film a controlled demolition of a model. Technicians might use a material called Primacord to achieve this effect. Primacord resembles a plastic rope and comes in various thicknesses up to 0.5 inches (1.3 mm) thick. Inside the cord is a high explosive. The thickness of the cord determines the strength of the explosion, and as it explodes, it cuts the things around it apart. So, technicians can place Primacord exactly where an object needs to come apart. The explosion happens quickly. When a technician ignites it, Primacord burns at a rate of 23,000 feet (7,000 m) per second. That's more than 4 miles (6.4 km) of Primacord in just one second!

The first atomic explosion, which J. Robert Oppenheimer and other scientists oversaw, occurred on July 16, 1945. Special effects pyrotechnicians have since been able to re-create lifelike imitations of such an explosion for films such as *Oppenheimer*.

Oppenheimer, Bombs, and Beyond

In 2023 Warner Brothers released *Oppenheimer*. The film follows the life and career of physicist J. Robert Oppenheimer, who was the director of the Manhattan Project, which created the first atomic bomb. Special effects technicians created the atomic explosion in the film using traditional pyrotechnic effects. Special effects supervisors Andrew Jackson and Scott Fisher created the illusion of a nuclear explosion using gasoline in mortars. After technicians fired the gasoline into the air, it vaporized and erupted into a large fireball resembling that of a nuclear blast—though, of course, much smaller. They added aluminum and magnesium powder to the gasoline, both of which burn with a bright, white light. This gave the impression of the intensely bright flash of light from an atomic bomb. Combined with miniature structures, the resulting explosion looked convincingly large and real.

Chapter 6

Fireworks Around the World

People worldwide have enjoyed fireworks for millennia. Audiences admire elaborate fireworks displays for their beauty, creativity, and the excitement they can lend to a celebration. Sometimes people or organizations hold fireworks displays to celebrate an important event in the history of a country, such as its independence, or displays might have a religious connection—celebrating the life of a saint, for instance. Other displays might be created solely as works of art to express the creativity of pyrotechnicians and pyrotechnics as an art form.

Fireworks for US Holidays

Fireworks have long been a part of the cultures of many nations. The Fourth of July in the United States would be almost unimaginable without fireworks displays. The idea of celebrating the holiday with fireworks goes back more than two hundred years. The day before the Declaration of Independence was signed in 1776, John Adams wrote a letter to his wife: "[This day] will be the most memorable . . . in the history of America.—I am apt to believe that it

In 1983 a fireworks display was held to celebrate the one-hundredth anniversary of the opening of New York City's Brooklyn Bridge.

will be celebrated, by succeeding generations, as the great anniversary festival. . . . It ought to be solemnized with pomp and parade . . . bonfires and illuminations [fireworks] from one end of this continent to the other from this time forward forever more."

Adams's prediction was accurate. The tradition of setting off fireworks for America's Independence Day began in Philadelphia on July 4, 1777, one year after the signing of the Declaration of Independence. The Sons of Liberty, a group most famous for having instigated the Boston Tea Party, organized a fireworks exhibition on the Boston Commons. *The Philadelphia Evening Post* described the event to its readers:

> Yesterday the 4th of July, being the anniversary of the Independence of the United States of America, was celebrated in this city with demonstrations of joy and festivity. About noon all the armed ships and gallies

> in the river were drawn up before the city, dressed in the gayest manner, with the colors of the United States and streamers displayed. At one o'clock, the yards being properly manned, they began the celebration of the day by a discharge of thirteen cannon from each of the ships, and one from each of the thirteen gallies, in honor of the Thirteen United States. . . . The evening was closed with the ringing of bells, and at night there was a grand exhibition of fireworks (which began and concluded with thirteen rockets) on the Commons, and the city was beautifully illuminated.

Today, the Fourth of July is celebrated with more than fourteen thousand fireworks displays across the United States. Americans spend close to $3 billion a year on fireworks. Since they have less restrictive laws, citizens in the South and Midwest spend nearly twice as much on fireworks as those in the rest of the country.

The Fourth, however, was not always a holiday celebrated with fireworks in all the states. In the South, fireworks—especially firecrackers—were originally reserved for celebrating Christmas. Setting off fireworks at Christmas remains a part of many Southern family traditions.

Guy Fawkes Day

In 1605 British soldier Guy Fawkes led the Gunpowder Plot—an attempt to assassinate the king and destroy the British government by blowing up Parliament. Fawkes had recently converted to Catholicism and was part of a group of Catholic conspirators who were unhappy with King James I for his failure to live up to his promise of religious tolerance. Fawkes was also an expert in fireworks. Fawkes and other conspirators smuggled thirty-six barrels of black powder into the cellar beneath the Palace of Westminster (the Houses of Parliament). (A legend suggests that the black powder had been purchased from one of the founders of Pains Fireworks, John Pain, whose family manufactured black

Christmas Crackers

The traditional British Christmas cracker comes in a package that looks like a paper tube covered in colorful paper twisted shut at both ends. When the end of the tube is pulled apart, a loud bang results. Often, a little poem, joke, paper crown, or small gift falls out. Sometimes two people will pull on opposite ends of the cracker. Two paper strips inside, coated with chemicals that react to the friction of being pulled apart, create the bang.

The packaging comes from candymaker Tom Smith, who in the 1850s began wrapping chocolates in paper tubes after seeing French bonbons wrapped in tissue paper that was twisted at either end. Inspired by the crackling sound of a log fire, he devised a way to have his chocolates also make a surprising bang when opened.

powder and fireworks.) This was over 2 tons (1.8 t) of black powder. The explosion of so much black powder would have destroyed any buildings within 130 feet (40 m) and damaged buildings up to 0.6 miles (900 m) away. Authorities discovered Fawkes in the cellar with matches in his hand, ready to light the fuse. He quickly confessed the plot and later named all his coconspirators. The suspects were tried, convicted, and executed for high treason. The failure of the Gunpowder Plot has been celebrated on November 5 every year since with—unsurprisingly—fireworks displays held across the nation.

Bastille Day

Every year on July 14, France celebrates the fall of the Bastille, a notorious state prison. It held not only criminals but political prisoners as well, many of whom had been imprisoned on the king's order. To many citizens, the Bastille symbolized the tyrannical rule of the monarchy, which Louis XVI led at the time. On July 14, 1789, a mob of protesters stormed the prison. They demanded the release of the prisoners. Soon the Bastille fell.

The fall of the Bastille signaled the beginning of the French Revolution and the end of the monarchy's domination. The French government declared the date a national holiday in 1880, and French citizens have traditionally celebrated with speeches, feasts, military ceremonies and, of course, fireworks. Although people hold displays around the country, the most spectacular shows occur in Paris around the Eiffel Tower. The performance can last for more than half an hour and lights up the city.

Diwali Fireworks in India

Diwali, also known as the Festival of Light, is a Hindu festival held every year between October and November, and it is one of the largest and most important holidays in India. Although Diwali had been celebrated in India for centuries before the Mongols, a group native to Mongolia, China, and parts of Russia, introduced black powder to the country, fireworks quickly became an important part of its festivities. In one village alone, nearly ten thousand people help manufacture fireworks for Diwali and other Indian festivals. Like Mexico, they undertake almost all this work in home workshops.

People celebrate Diwali with many types of fireworks, but firecrackers are especially popular. Besides using them on holidays, people once used firecrackers to control insect pests in rice fields. The burning powder in firecrackers emits sulfur fumes, which repel insects.

Since the 2010s several cities in India have initiated bans on fireworks due to concerns about pollution, but these have always met with strong protests and have either been ignored or soon repealed. In

Experts estimate that more than 50,000 tons (45,359 t) of fireworks are set off to celebrate Diwali each year.

2017 the Supreme Court of India banned all fireworks in the National Capital Region, which includes the capital city of Delhi. The National Green Tribunal, a legal body that deals with environmental cases, initiated this ban. Elsewhere in the country, cities have taken other initiatives. In 2019 India's Council for Scientific and Industrial Research developed a "green" firecracker. It contains fewer dangerous elements, such as barium, and also makes less noise.

Omagari Fireworks Festival, Japan

The Omagari Fireworks Festival is a fireworks competition held in Daisen, a city in the Akita Prefecture of Japan. The Suwa Shrine, a Shinto shrine in Nagasaki, Japan, first organized it in 1910. Each year, more than seven hundred thousand visitors attend the festival to watch as more than twenty fireworks manufacturers compete in Japan's national fireworks competition.

The festival typically consists of three categories for contestants to compete in, including daytime fireworks and creative fireworks. Daytime fireworks use colored smoke instead of light effects to achieve patterns in the sky. Patterns in colors such as red, yellow, blue, green, and purple might create peonies, chrysanthemums, and other patterns. Creative fireworks sync fireworks to music. Judges score fireworks based on their design and use of color.

Fireworks and Religion

For generations, people in Mexico have traditionally celebrated days honoring saints with fireworks. For example, St. John of God, a monk from the 1500s, braved a fire to save the patients in his hospital and later became the patron saint of the impoverished and sick. Fireworks makers also came to view him as their protective figure. People celebrate the Feast of St. John in honor of St. John of God each year on March 8. Beginning in the 1800s, residents of Tultepec, a town near Mexico City, celebrated the holiday by making bulls out of papier-mâché, called toritos, or "little bulls." People fill these papier-mâché bulls with fireworks. Celebrants sometimes carry toritos

Toritos are often colorful and may feature designs such as floral patterns on the outside.

on their shoulders before igniting them in the streets. People might also build castillos, or "castles"—large structures made of wood and bamboo and covered in fireworks—to honor saints.

More than three thousand festivals are celebrated in Mexico every year with pyrotechnics. In addition to the Feast of St. John of God, among the most important are Mexico's Independence Day, which is celebrated on September 16, and the celebration of the Virgin of Guadalupe on December 12. A quarter of a million people might crowd into Mexico City's central plaza to witness these festive fireworks displays. Mexico also hosts the annual Feria Nacional de la Pirotecnia (National Pyrotechnics Festival). It's in Tultepec, lasts for nine days, and attracts over one hundred thousand people each year.

Thai Rocket Festival

In Thailand, many festivals center on rockets. Bun Bang Fai is held every year in many towns and villages in northeast Thailand. *Bun* means "merit," *bang* refers to the bamboo tubes that the rockets are made of, and *fai* means "fire." People launch rockets during the festival to honor Phaya Thaen, the god of the rain. Historically, they did this to ensure that there would be rain to bring a successful rice harvest. The rockets are colorfully decorated, often with a figure of a naga, a giant serpent from Buddhist tradition. They are also large, containing 44 to 55 pounds (20 to 25 kg) of black powder. A completed rocket may weigh as much as 265 pounds (120 kg), be up to 30 feet (9 m) long, and travel several miles through the sky. Teams of participants compete in tournaments to see which rockets travel the longest distance or reach the tallest heights. These rockets can be dangerous since no one knows which way they may travel or how far. Unsurprisingly, many people believe that if a rocket lands on a house, that house will be cursed with bad luck.

Bun Bang Fai is held annually in May or June and attracts tens of thousands of visitors. Aside from rocket launchings, visitors can enjoy traditional folk dancing, music, food, and parades.

Laos, a neighboring country to Thailand, holds similar festivals featuring rockets. Chinese people who live near the border of Thailand

and Laos and ethnic Pa'O people in Myanmar also celebrate festivals with rockets.

Lunar New Year

In China, people greet the Lunar New Year with fireworks. Historically, people used firecrackers to ward away evil spirits such as Nian, a beast that appeared on Lunar New Year's Eve to eat villagers and destroy homes. The loud popping and crackling noises that bamboo made would scare the Nian off.

Lunar New Year celebrations typically last fifteen days, beginning on the new moon of the Lunar New Year and ending with the following full moon. Many families set off fireworks at midnight as the new year begins, and on that morning, they set off firecrackers before leaving the house to ensure good luck for the coming year.

Red is considered a lucky color in Chinese culture. That's why most, if not all, firecrackers made in that country are wrapped in red paper. During Lunar New Year celebrations, shredded red paper covers streets all over the country. The debris is usually left for a few days since sweeping it up right away might also sweep away all the good luck the firecrackers brought.

International Festivals and Competitions

Every year, organizations hold contests around the world in which fireworks manufacturers compete to see who can create the most spectacular, beautiful, and original displays. The largest fireworks competition in the world is L'International des Feux Loto-Québec, or the Montreal Fireworks Festival, in Canada, which has been held since 1985. Fireworks companies from around the world send teams to compete for the top prizes. Eight or nine final teams end up in the competition. They then receive a theme for the competition and must create a fireworks display that illustrates that theme. Upward of three million people flock to Montreal to witness the event, which runs for nearly a month from late June to late July annually. As many as six thousand fireworks might go off during each half-hour show.

The launching of the giant rockets during the Bun Bang Fai festival is a spectacular event.

Besides the Montreal Fireworks Festival, other international competitions include the World Fireworks Championship, hosted by the city of Blackpool in England; the International Fireworks Competition, held in Hanover, Germany; and the Philippine International Pyromusical Competition (formerly known as the World Pyro Olympics), held in Manila, the capital of the Philippines. One of the challenges that the five-day Philippine festival sets is that the displays need to be coordinated with music.

In 1966 the Mediterranean nation of Monaco began hosting the Monaco Art en Ciel (Art in the Sky), otherwise known as the International Pyromelodic Fireworks Competition. Each summer for two days in July and two days in August, pyrotechnicians from all over the world enter their art into the competition. A committee of judges selects four entrants for the final public show. Spectators can vote online to decide which of the four wins a prize. In 1979 the Grucci company took first place at the competition. It was the first American fireworks company to receive the coveted gold medal. Beginning in 1996, the festival began combining music and fireworks. Entrants seek to perfectly sync music with their pyrotechnics.

Chapter 7

Fireworks as a Hobby

Many people enjoy making fireworks as a hobby. But as you might imagine, working with fireworks can be dangerous and should be with adult or professional supervision. One of the first things anyone should do before taking up fireworks as a hobby is to join an organization such as the Pyrotechnics Guild International or the Junior Pyrotechnics Association (JPA). The PGI is a global nonprofit organization made up of amateur and professional adult fireworks enthusiasts. Founded in 1969, the PGI has more than sixteen hundred members, publishes a bulletin, and holds a weeklong convention every year in early August. In addition to published bulletins, the PGI has online discussion groups where members can ask questions and share information and experiences. One of the first goals of the PGI is to "promote safe and responsible use and display of fireworks."

The JPA is associated with the PGI and is specifically intended for people between the ages of six and seventeen who want to learn how to handle and use fireworks safely and legally. Working under the close supervision of experienced hobbyists and fireworks professionals, JPA members learn how to plan, set up, and safely

The PGI convention features a mix of regular fireworks displays and pyromusicals.

shoot public fireworks displays. They gain hands-on experience from working side by side with a parent, guardian, or other responsible adult. The JPA holds a convention at the same time and place as the PGI every year. During conventions, the JPA holds seminars and workshops to help train members in techniques and safety. They also present a full-scale consumer fireworks display on one of the nights.

In addition to the PGI, which is an international organization, people can find many regional clubs with similar activities around the country. Like the PGI and JPA, their focus is on safety and fun.

Keeping Safe

The American Pyrotechnics Safety and Education Foundation aims to help people, especially young people, understand how to use fireworks safely and appropriately. This can help reduce the number of

Fireworks Safety

Here are some tips to help stay safe while lighting fireworks:

- Always use fireworks outside and have a bucket of water or a hose nearby in case of accidents.
- Designate a safety perimeter. If you have ground-based fireworks such as fountains, keep spectators at least 35 feet (11 m) away. For aerial fireworks, you'll want everyone to move around 150 feet (46 m) back.
- Sometimes a firework won't go off. Never try to relight a failed firework. Let it sit for five to ten minutes before you approach the firework and put it in a bucket of water. This can prevent injury from a delayed explosion and disarm the firework permanently so you can safely dispose of it later.
- Don't allow young children to handle sparklers. Sparklers burn at about 2,000°F (1,093°C)—hot enough to melt some metals. Sparklers can ignite clothing or cause severe burns.
- Fireworks—especially noisy ones—can be extremely stressful for pets. Keep your pets indoors. Close the curtains or blinds and turn on a TV or radio to provide some cover noise and distraction. Toys or treats may also help distract them from the fireworks.
- Soak both used and unused fireworks in water for several hours before discarding.
- Never place a part of your body directly over a firework or hold a firework in your hand when lighting it.
- Never try to take apart, open up, or change a firework in any way.
- Only light one firework at a time. Lighting multiple fireworks at the same time increases the risk of accidents occurring from fuses burning faster than expected or designed.
- Purchase fireworks only from reputable dealers.
- Follow the directions on the firework exactly.
- Avoid alcohol or drugs when handling or using fireworks.

fireworks-related accidents and injuries. In addition to these efforts, the foundation warns both young people and adults about the dangers of using illegal fireworks, or those that don't meet Consumer Product Safety Commission standards.

There are several ways to tell whether a firework is illegal—and probably unsafe. Legitimate fireworks will have the manufacturer's name, the country of origin, warning labels, and instructions on how to use the firework. The firework will also have "DOT Consumer Fireworks 1.4G" printed somewhere on it, as the Department of Transportation (DOT) regulates consumer fireworks and classifies them as division 1.4G hazardous materials, meaning they are explosive objects with a low explosion risk. Illegal fireworks will have none of these. If a firework was bought on the street and not from a licensed shop or vendor, it is probably illegal. Responsible pyrotechnics hobbyists may set off their own fireworks to show them to others, but they never sell or share the fireworks they have made.

Collecting Fireworks Art

Many people collect fireworks as a hobby. This is called *pyrobilia*, meaning "love of fireworks." Collector Brian Zompanti coined the term. But this hobby needs to be done cautiously, since fireworks are always potentially dangerous and need to be carefully stored and cared for.

A popular version of this hobby that is both safe and fun is collecting fireworks labels. When firecrackers were first introduced to the United States, most came from China.

Fireworks labels often feature bright colors and interesting art and patterns.

Themes such as robots, rockets, and spacecraft have long been popular for fireworks labels.

The first shipments arrived in wooden crates. These crates usually had an attractive, colorful label attached that enabled a storeowner to use the crate as a display. The packages of firecrackers in the crate, however, were usually wrapped in plain red paper. As firecrackers became more popular, manufacturers wanted to find ways to attract customers and distinguish one brand from another. So they started putting individual labels on each pack of firecrackers.

The first labels featured Chinese themes such as animals, flowers, or dragons, but as the US market expanded, companies created labels to specifically appeal to American consumers. The labels became more colorful and featured themes such as cowboys and soldiers, and characters such as Davy Crockett. Rockets, spaceships, and astronauts are also common. Animals have long been a popular theme for firecracker labels, even if the choice of animal seems to make no sense. For example, we have had brands called Giraffe, Fish, and even Lobster firecrackers. We've also had stranger brands, such as Typewriter. There have been more than a thousand different brands of firecrackers, all with their own unique label.

One of the difficulties in collecting firecracker labels is that the product is made to be blown up. One easy way around this is to remove the label before using the firework. Another way to grow a collection is through trading or purchasing labels from other collectors. Many people collect firecracker labels.

Another possible hobby is to collect items associated with fireworks. Many fireworks companies sell merchandise such as T-shirts, hats, stickers, and even pickleball paddles featuring company logos and other art.

Fireworks and the Environment

Like many things that are both fun and beautiful, fireworks have a downside: They are not very good for the environment. One might think it is all the smoke that is the problem, adding to the carbon in the atmosphere. But the typical fireworks display doesn't add any more carbon to the environment than an automobile traveling 20 miles (32 km). The real problem stems from the beautiful colors.

Many of the colors you see when a shell explodes in the night sky are created by chemicals in the black powder. While many color-producing elements are safe for the environment—such as calcium, sodium, and magnesium—many others can be dangerous or toxic. Cadmium, for instance, is a known carcinogen—a substance that produces cancers in humans. In addition to these potentially harmful elements, fireworks also create particulates, or microscopic, dustlike particles of solid matter. Particulates can accumulate in the lungs and bloodstream, potentially causing health issues from cancer and lung diseases to strokes.

Since the smoke from a large fireworks display can linger for days, the effects can be far-reaching. And since many of the chemicals used in fireworks don't decompose easily, they can remain in the soil and water for years or even decades. Even the debris from the cardboard and paper casings can be a problem. In addition to the charcoal contained in the black powder, the paper, cardboard, plastic, and glues used in the casing containing the firework all add carbon to the environment when they burn.

And all fireworks need an oxidizer to burn. This is any substance that provides oxygen. One of the most common oxidizers used in fireworks are perchlorates, or chemical compounds rich in oxygen. Perchlorates contain chlorine, a chemical found in many swimming pools that kills bacteria. Chlorine enhances the color of many fireworks, but it also produces carcinogenic compounds when the firework burns. Unfortunately, burning perchlorates releases such dangerous pollutants into the air, which eventually make their way into lakes and rivers.

Even the ordinary sparkler can be hazardous to the environment. Most sparklers use a form of barium called barium nitrate as an oxidizer. This releases barium, a highly toxic heavy metal, which settles on any nearby surface . . . including food. Since barium is water-soluble, humans easily ingest it. It can cause severe abdominal pain, abnormal blood pressure, and even paralysis.

To help combat these dangers, many fireworks manufacturers are trying to change how fireworks are made and used. Disneyland and Disney World are famous for their nightly fireworks shows. In a single year, the theme parks use more than one million fireworks. Instead of using the traditional black powder-fueled mortars to launch the aerial shells, the parks have switched to mortars using compressed air.

"Green" fireworks such as India's green firecracker are also an option. This doesn't mean that the fireworks look green but rather that they are less harmful to the environment. Fireworks manufacturers have been switching from perchlorates to nitrogen-based oxidizers. These release fewer harmful chemicals into the atmosphere, causing less pollution. Unfortunately, many of these oxidizers are much more expensive than the traditional ones, so they aren't as common yet. And since there is little government oversight regulating the use of toxic chemicals in fireworks, most fireworks manufacturers have little incentive to turn to more expensive ingredients.

Still, there is a growing number of fireworks manufacturers who are making an effort to address the problem of pollution. A German company, Weco, has turned to using largely recycled paper and biodegradable plastic in its casings. Howards Fireworks, an Australian company, has made a commitment to reducing its impact on the environment by using recycled materials and reusable products wherever possible. Britain's Pains Fireworks company is also committed to reducing its impact on the environment, making sure that every event is carbon neutral (it uses or absorbs as much carbon as it releases into the atmosphere). In India, where firecrackers have long been an important part of the festivals celebrating Vijayadashami and Diwali, officials have been trying to reduce both air and noise pollution with little success so far.

Conclusion

The Future of Fireworks

As we discussed, environmental concerns are, of course, one of the issues facing the fireworks industry. Though many fireworks contain toxic materials, especially the metallic elements used to create bright colors, there is much debate on just how much fireworks contribute to air and water pollution. People are also concerned about noise pollution and safety.

Every year about ten thousand or more people in the United States are treated in emergency wards for injuries related to fireworks. Of the consumer fireworks the Consumer Product Safety Commission tested in 2023, 43 percent did not comply with legal standards. Some failed tests because the fireworks included prohibited chemicals and others because the fireworks were overloaded with black powder. Consumers should purchase recognized brands from reputable dealers and then use the product carefully and according to instructions.

Concerns about fireworks have led some people to search for alternatives. Laser shows were an early alternative. But even these have safety concerns. When used indoors, great care needs to be

People typically wear white during Holi. The color has symbolic significance, but it also serves as a good canvas for the festival's brightly colored powders.

taken to be sure that none of the lasers will point into anyone's eyes. The powerful light can cause permanent damage. When used outdoors, lasers can interfere with aircraft flying overhead.

People can use confetti, colorful powder, glow sticks, silly string, or even bubbles in place of fireworks such as sparklers and fountains. Outdoor confetti cannons—powered by compressed air—can launch colorful bursts of biodegradable paper. People can achieve a similar effect using colored powders that create clouds of bright colors. Using colored powder as a substitute for fireworks was probably inspired by Holi, a Hindu festival held every spring in India. It's also known as the Festival of Colors, and people celebrate it by throwing handfuls of brightly colored powder into the air.

Glow sticks are plastic tubes that contain chemicals that glow brightly when combined. The glow might last for up to twenty-four hours, though more often it's only between eight and twelve hours. The light is cold, and the chemicals are generally nontoxic. Glow sticks, however, are not biodegradable and need to be disposed of properly.

One alternative to fireworks that is growing in popularity is aerial performances of drones. A drone show might consist of hundreds of individual drones that a computer carefully programs and controls. Drones are equipped with multicolored lights and can perform complex dances in the sky and create elaborate patterns and shapes, including everything from company logos to animated dragons. Some large drone shows have employed thousands of drones. In December 2023 a company called Sky Elements Drones launched 1,499 drones to create a three-dimensional, 700-foot-tall (213 m) Santa Claus over a Texas football stadium. The largest drone show occurred in China in 2024, with more than ten thousand drones.

One experimental idea is cloud projection, a type of laser show where lasers project images onto low-lying clouds. This has been done with some success in Japan and England. But developers face two problems. One is the potential danger of a laser interfering with an

Laser shows can feature just as many stunning colors as fireworks but are better for the environment.

aircraft passing overhead, and another very important one is the need for a cloudy day.

People have also experimented with "electronic firecrackers." These attempt to duplicate the effect of a firecracker with an electronic flash and loud crackling or popping sound. These aren't popular alternatives, because they are more expensive than traditional firecrackers and the final effect is a poor imitation.

Are fireworks ever going to go away? Probably not. Besides being around for more than a thousand years, fireworks are immensely popular all over the world. They are also an important part of many traditions, cultures, and religions. Outright bans on fireworks have rarely been successful. The truth is that nothing can really substitute for the sound, sight, and even smell of traditional fireworks.

GLOSSARY

aerial shell: a fireworks device designed to be launched into the air during a fireworks display

barrage: a set of aerial fireworks set off in rapid succession

black powder: also known as gunpowder, a fast-burning mixture of sulfur, charcoal, and potassium nitrate that includes a fuel and an oxidizer that turn into a large volume of gas almost instantly when ignited

bursting charge: the charge of black powder in an aerial shell that scatters the final effect; also called a break charge

cake: also called a barrage, a firework that consists of several smaller fireworks bundled together

Catherine wheel: a disk-shaped firework with small, rocketlike devices attached to the rim that cause it to spin rapidly when ignited

comet: a pellet that produces a long trail of sparks when shot individually from a mortar or in a group from a shell

consumer fireworks: fireworks that are intended for the consumer. The permitted usage of consumer fireworks varies by state. Examples include fountains, cones, and firecrackers.

deflagration: burning very rapidly

detonator: a small, explosive device used to set off high explosives

display fireworks: large fireworks designed to produce visible or audible effects for entertainment

firecracker: a small pyrotechnic device, consisting of a paper tube containing a small amount of black powder and perhaps flash paper or flash powder, that creates a flash and loud noise

flare: a pyrotechnic device intended to create a bright white or colored light

flash paper: a thin sheet of paper treated with acid. It disappears almost instantly in a flash of flame when ignited.

flash powder: mixtures that contain a perchlorate with powdered aluminum or a magnesium and aluminum alloy that, when ignited, result in a loud explosion and flash of light

fountain: a device that projects a spray of sparks

fuse: a paper or fiber tube or cable containing a combustible substance meant to set off an explosive charge by transmitting fire to it

gerb: a firework that creates a jet of sparks lasting between fifteen and sixty seconds. They can be used as fountains by themselves or as the drivers on a Catherine wheel. The word comes from the French word *grebe*, meaning "a sheaf of wheat," which the firework resembles.

Greek fire: an ancient Greek weapon consisting of petroleum, sulfur, resin, and pitch. Set on fire, it could be ejected by a pump onto an enemy.

lifting charge: the composition that propels the pyrotechnic device into the air

mortar: a heavy fiberglass or steel tube that contains an explosive charge used to launch fireworks into the air

oxidizer: any compound that provides oxygen for combustion

perchlorates: chemical compounds that provide oxygen for combustion

potassium nitrate: also known as saltpeter (KNO_3), an oxidizer used in making black powder

Primacord: a ropelike cord of detonating material

pyrotechnician: a person who designs or handles fireworks

pyrotechnics: the art of manufacturing and designing fireworks

Roman candle: a chain-fused firework that propels a series of aerial shell or comet effects into the air from a single tube

sparkler: a heavy, metal wire coated with a substance that gives off showers of sparks while burning

squib: a small, firecracker-like device often used to simulate bullet hits

stars: fireworks materials that are compressed into small cubes or round pellets. They are part of aerial shells and create flashes of light, sparks, or bangs.

SOURCE NOTES

9 "twisting and turning . . . or charring them": Alan St. Hill Brock, *Pyrotechnics* (Daniel O'Connor, 1922), 13.

10 "Chinese snow": Ahmad Y. al-Hassan, "Potassium Nitrate in Arabic and Latin Sources," History of Science and Technology in Islam, accessed March 12, 2025, http://www.history-science-technology.com/articles/articles%203.html.

11 "Annis arabum 630 . . . si scias artificium,": Henry W. L. Hine, *Gunpowder and Ammunition* (Longmans, Green, 1904), 156.

11–12 "From the force . . . brilliancy of lightning": Roger Bacon, *The Opus Majus of Roger Bacon*, vol. 2, trans. Robert Belle Burke (Russell & Russell, 1962), 629.

12 "by the flash . . . or endure it": Petar Bojani, "Terrorism: Terror and Explosion," Centre for Modern Thought, University of Aberdeen, accessed March 12, 2025, https://www.abdn.ac.uk/media/site/modernthought/content-images/bojanic_terror.pdf.

13 "one pound of . . . with iron wire": James Riddick Partington, *A History of Greek Fire and Gunpowder* (Johns Hopkins University Press, 1999), 49.

15 "the King would . . . or firework": William Shakespeare, *Love's Labor's Lost*, Folger Shakespeare Library, accessed March 12, 2025, https://www.folger.edu/explore/shakespeares-works/loves-labors-lost/read/.

15 "If any person . . . to the poor": Megan Brittan, "Fireworks," eighteenthcenturylit, last updated March 16, 2017, http://eighteenthcenturylit.pbworks.com/w/page/112486969/Fireworks.

15 "throwing squibs, serpents, and other fireworks": Brittan.

16 "two men in . . . of the show": "Page: Pyrotechnics the History and Art of Firework Making (1922).djvu/58," WikiSource, last updated March 13, 2021, https://en.m.wikisource.org/wiki/Page:Pyrotechnics_the_history_and_art_of_firework_making_(1922).djvu/58.

18 "There appeared for . . . still admired today.": Brock, *Pyrotechnics*, 21.

20 "fireworks display, formerly . . . adventures, unexpected scenes": Émile Magne, quoted in Ron Miller, "The First Fireworks Displays Were Terrifyingly Huge," Gizmodo, July 7, 2014, https://gizmodo.com/the-first-fireworks-displays-were-terrifyingly-huge-1600541130.

21 "the repetition of . . . tedious to all": Brock, *Pyrotechnics*, 41.

21 "on a scale . . . in the trade": Brock, 47.

22 "wildefire woorkes": Thomas Harriot, A *Briefe and True Report of the New Found Land of Virginia*, trans. Richard Hacklvit (New York, 1871), 27.

28 "We're using everything . . . in the sky.": "Biggest Fireworks Show Planned at Bridge," *New York Times*, May 23, 1983, https://www.nytimes.com/1983/05/23/nyregion/biggest-fireworks-show-planned-at-bridge.html.

49 "mischievous use of pyrotechnics": Jennie Cohen, "Fireworks' Vibrant History," History.com, last updated March 29, 2023, https://www.history.com/news/fireworks-vibrant-history.

72–73 "[This day] will . . . forward forever more.": John Adams, quoted in "Letter from John Adams to Abigal Adams, 3 July 1776," Massachusetts Historical Society, accessed March 10, 2025, https://www.masshist.org/database/102.

73–74 "Yesterday the 4th . . . was beautifully illuminated.": Historical Society of Pennsylvania, *The Pennsylvania Magazine of History and Biography* 35 (Historical Society of Pennsylvania, 1911), 372–373.

82 "promote safe and . . . display of fireworks": "Welcome to the PGI! Pyrotechnics Guild International," Pyrotechnics Guild International, accessed March 10, 2025, https://pgi.org/.

SELECTED BIBLIOGRAPHY

Brock, Alan St. Hill. *Pyrotechnics: The History and Art of Firework Making*. Daniel O'Connor, 1922.

Carr, Kevin Matthew. "A Theater of the Senses: A Cultural History of Theatrical Effects in Early-Modern England." PhD diss., Florida State University, 2013.

"Home." American Pyrotechnics Safety and Education Foundation. Accessed March 12, 2025. https://www.celebratesafely.org/.

"100 Years of Sparks the Story About American Fireworks." YouTube video, 12:26. Posted by Sam Angello, January 11, 2016. https://www.youtube.com/watch?v=6yhtO6uIA_4.

"Pyrotechnic Records and Interesting Facts." Firework Safety. Accessed March 12, 2025. https://www.fireworksafety.com/.

Rickitt, Richard. *Special Effects: The History and Technique*. Billboard Books, 2006.

Rocker, Megan. *How It Happens at the Fireworks Factory*. Clara House Books, 2004.

Sharpe, Mitchell R. *Development of the Lifesaving Rocket: A Study in 19th Century Technological Fallout.* George C. Marshall Space Flight Center, 1969.

"Skylighter—Pyrotechnic Chemicals and Supplies, Sparklers, Fireworks." Skylighter. Accessed March 12, 2025. https://www.skylighter.com/.

Theatre Effects. *Special Effects with Fire and Smoke: A Technical Manual.* Theatre Effects, 1985.

Wilkie, Bernard. *Creating Special Effects for TV and Video.* Focal, 1996.

FURTHER INFORMATION

Books

Cobb, Vicki. *Fireworks.* Lerner Publications, 2006.

DeVincent Hayes, Gianni. *Zambelli, The First Family of Fireworks: A Story of Global Success.* Paul S. Eriksson, 2003.

Dotz, Warren. *Firecrackers! An Eye-Popping Collection of Chinese Firework Art.* Ten Speed, 2008.

Dotz, Warren. *Firecrackers: The Art and History.* Ten Speed, 2000.

Otto, Caroline. *Celebrate Chinese New Year.* National Geographic Kids, 2015.

Plimpton, George. *Fireworks.* Doubleday, 1984.

Werrett, Simon. *Fireworks: Pyrotechnic Arts and Sciences in European History.* University of Chicago Press, 2010.

Websites

Brocks Fireworks

https://www.brocksfireworks.com/

The official site of one of the world's oldest fireworks companies offers information about their history, how to safely dispose of expired fireworks, and more.

Fireworks Clubs and Organizations

https://www.usfireworks.biz/clubs.htm

US Fireworks offers a list of national and regional fireworks clubs along with their contact information.

Fireworks Laws by State 2025

https://worldpopulationreview.com/state-rankings/fireworks-laws-by-state

World Population Review provides an interactive US map of fireworks laws that were active in 2025.

Junior Pyrotechnic Association (JPA)

https://pgi.org/pages/junior-pyros/

The JPA is dedicated to youth between the ages of six and seventeen who attend the PGI convention. This page explains how to join.

Pyrotechnics Guild International (PGI)

https://pgi.org/

The PGI is a worldwide group of pyrotechnic enthusiasts. Their website hosts information about the guild, membership, and the PGI convention.

Zambelli Fireworks

https://www.zambellifireworks.com/

Zambelli Fireworks Company is one of the largest fireworks companies worldwide. Their official site explains their history, the types of shows they put on, and more.

Pyrotechnics Clubs

This is by no means a complete list. Search online for your local club. Most clubs have shoots, in which members can participate, and host seminars on safety and training in setting up and firing professional fireworks displays.

Bluegrass Pyrotechnic Guild

https://www.bluegrasspyrotechnicguild.com/

Heartland Pyrotechnic Arts Association

https://www.heartlandpyro.org/

Iowa Pyrotechnic Association

https://www.iowapyro.com/

Michigan Pyrotechnic Arts Guild

https://mpag.org/web/

Mid-Atlantic Fireworks Club

https://www.crackerjacks.org/

Midlands Pyrotechnic Association

http://midlandspyroassociation.com/

National Fireworks Association
https://www.nationalfireworks.com/

New Hampshire Pyrotechnic Association
https://nhpyrotechnics.org/

Northeast Ohio Pyrotechnics Group
https://www.neopg.com/

Northern Lighter Pyrotechnics
https://www.northernlighters.org/

Northwest Pyrotechnics Association
https://www.npaclub.org/

Ohio Pyrotechnic Arts Guild
http://www.opag.us/

Pyrotechnic Artists of Texas
https://fireants.org/

Rocky Mountain Pyrotechnics Guild
https://rmpg.org/

Tennessee Fireworks Association
http://www.tnfwa.org/

Western New York Pyrotechnic Association
https://www.wnypa.org/

Western Pyrotechnic Association
https://www.westernpyro.org/

Wisconsin Pyrotechnic Arts Guild
https://www.wpag.us/

ACKNOWLEDGMENTS

Special thanks to the following:

- Hank Atterbury, for advice and images relating to motion picture pyrotechnic effects
- Ryan Francisco, Francisco Display Fireworks, https://franciscodisplayfireworks.com, for information and images about the profession of pyrotechnics and the creation of public fireworks displays
- William F. Albus, Lotus Fireworks and Museum, https://www.lotusfireworks.com, for historic fireworks images
- Roberto Sorgi, https://americanfireworks.com, for information about the manufacture of consumer and display fireworks
- Phil Grucci, Grucci Fireworks, https://www.grucci.com, for information about the company and its history
- Guy Deeker, Pains Fireworks, https://www.painsfireworks.com, for providing historic and contemporary images
- Frank Winter, https://www.frankhwinter.com, for information regarding the Thai rocket festivals
- Diwerent, https://www.diwerent.com, for permission to use images of the Thai rocket festival
- Comet Marine, https://www.comet-marine.com, for information on lifesaving rockets and flares
- PainsWessex, https://www.painswessex.com, for information on lifesaving rockets and flares
- Will Wallus, Event Horizon, http://www.precisionenergetics.co.uk/, for information and images relating to motion picture pyrotechnics
- John Ellis, for providing images and valuable insights into motion picture pyrotechnics
- Brendan Calton, https://www.pyrobilia.com, for access to his extensive collection of fireworks art
- Spirit of '76, https://76fireworks.com, for use of images depicting the manufacture of fireworks
- Warren Klofkorn, for providing access to his collection of books and memorabilia
- Precocious Pyrotecnics, https://precociouspyro.com/index.html, for providing images and information about fireworks manufacturing.
- YOVON Fireworks & Firecrackers Machine Factory, for providing images of fireworks-making machinery

INDEX

ABOUT THE AUTHOR

Ron Miller is an author and illustrator specializing in science and science fiction. He is the author of more than seventy books, many of them award-winning. He has also designed postage stamps and worked on motion pictures.

PHOTO ACKNOWLEDGMENTS

Image credits: Manjurul Haque/Alamy, p. 5; Wellcome Collection, p. 7; Codex Skylitzes Matritensis, Biblioteca Nacional de Madrid, p. 10; Library of Congress, pp. 11, 25, 41, 73, 89; John Bate via Public Domain Review, p. 16; Menigault Bernard/Alamy, p. 17; American Fireworks via Ron Miller, pp. 27, 31; © Ron Miller, pp. 33, 35, 47, 69; Jörn Petring/picture-alliance/dpa/AP Images, p. 36; Francisco Fireworks via Ron Miller, p. 44; Chris Howes/Wild Places Photography/Alamy, p. 47; RGB Ventures/SuperStock/Alamy, p. 50; Jane Barlow - PA Images via Getty Images, p. 53; Agnat/Wikimedia Commons (CC BY-SA 4.0), p. 55; Fred Ordway IV via Ron Miller, p. 57; Frank Albert Charles Burke/Fairfax Media via Getty Images, p. 59; Courtesy of Ron Miller (Public Domain), pp. 60, 75, 85; Gisela Schober/Getty Images, p. 63; Søren Haraldsted via Ron Miller, p. 65; AP Photo, p. 71; Umang Gajjar/Getty Images, p. 77; RONALDO SCHEMIDT/AFP via Getty Images, p. 78; Diwerent.com via Ron Miller p. 81; AP Photo/Butler Eagle, Dave Prelosky, p. 83; National Air and Space Museum via Ron Miller, p. 86 (left); Courtesy of Ron Miller, p. 86 (right); Paddy Photography/Getty Images, p. 91; Photo Spirit/Shutterstock, p. 92. Design elements/Front Cover: enjoynz/Getty Images; nicepix/Shutterstock.